# Easygoing
## ENTERTAINING

### THE "HARRY'S WILD ABOUT YOU!" COOKBOOK
by
### HARRY SCHWARTZ

*Seaside Publishing, Inc.*
*St. Petersburg, Florida*

Copyright 1995 Harry W. Schwartz

All rights reserved under International Pan American Copyright Convention including the right of reproduction in whole or in part in any form. No part of this book may be reproduced or transmitted in any form or by any means, electronic or mechanical, including photocopying, recording, or by any information storage and retrieval system, without permission in writing from the publisher.

Published by SeaSide Publishing, Inc.
For additional information or copies, contact
Seaside Publishing, Post Office Box 14441,
St. Petersburg, FL 33733

Manufactured in the United States of America
Member of the Publishers Association of the South

ISBN: 0-942084-86-1

**Cover Design by Byron Kennedy**

**Typesetting and Design by Susan Fosset**

Edited by Joyce LaFray

# TABLE OF CONTENTS

| | |
|---|---|
| Preface | 1 |
| Chapter I: *Artistic Surroundings - Setting the Table* | 2 |
| Chapter II: *The Great Outdoors - Entertaining Outside* | 5 |
| Chapter III: *Elegant, Easy, and Light* | 28 |
| Chapter IV: *The Cocktail Buffet* | 86 |
| Chapter V: *Soups, Pasta and One Dish Meals* | 145 |
| Chapter VI: *Breads, Cookies, Cakes and Pastries* | 173 |
| Chapter VII: *The Influence of the Orient* | 202 |
| Chapter VIII: *The Influence of the Southwest* | 242 |
| Chapter IX: *Limited Engagements* | 268 |
| Acknowledgements | 278 |
| Source List | 279 |
| Glossary | 281 |
| Chef's Notes | 284 |

# PREFACE

It has often been said that behind every good man there is a good woman. In my life, nothing could be more true. My wife Laurie is not only my best friend, but also my valuable helper. Not only does she manage all of our shopping chores and our young daughter, but she is a significant source of inspiration. While I gather all of the glory from our many-faceted culinary escapades, Laurie manages to help it happen with style and ease.

Ever since I was young, entertaining has been an integral part of my life. My mother, an exceptional hostess, always made certain that things were done right. She took the utmost care in setting the table, regardless of whether we were using paper plates or fine bone china. She garnished plates with fresh flowers long before it was avant-garde. Her table decorations were superb works of art; frequent exclamations by guests were not uncommon. Mother never failed to include me in her preparations, allowing me to perform important chores as well as those that were considered trivial. Working with Mother was always a joy.

Next to Mother, a talented friend and chef, Melva Bucksbaum, showed me the joys of culinary highs by encouraging me to teach cooking classes. She introduced me to the famous French cooking school, *La Varenne Ecole de la Cuisine* in Paris, France, and to Bugialli, the famed Italian chef. She surprised me with *Entertaining* by Martha Stewart long before Ms. Stewart was a household word. While entertaining became an enjoyable activity, eating became a magnificent ritual. At a very early age I realized that creating and enjoying good food was one of my favorite pleasures.

Today, I am still wild about preparing a fabulous meal and sharing it with family and friends. I have always felt that preparation of these meals should be an easygoing experience — not an endless chore that keeps you in the kitchen for hour upon hour. *Easygoing Entertaining*: that's the way it should be — a ceremonial ritual of sorts, where there is plenty of time for sharing, caring, celebrating, relaxing and best of all, enjoying!

I hope you enjoy these recipes as much as I have enjoyed creating them.

*Fondly, Harry*

*Chapter I*

# ARTISTIC SURROUNDINGS
## Setting the Table

Setting the table sets the stage. It is an integral part of the preparations and often the first thing your guests will note. First impressions are important. Enhancing your table will not only glorify the experience but make it pleasant. Working with beautiful things makes tablesetting an art. It is also easy to do ahead of time.

You need not spend a great deal of money to have an attractive table. Picking up an antique table cloth and unique napkins for ten dollars at a garage sale just takes a little extra time. For sure, finding an interesting set of crystal glasses or attractive plates does not require a fat checkbook, but merely a discovering eye.

We have limited ourselves to certain styles and periods. When at antique shows, we search for vendors selling their tarnished silver items by the ounce. We look for odd-numbered sets such as nine glasses or ten plates; usually one gets a better deal. Carefully and lovingly mixing plates, glasses, and silver not only makes for a more beautiful and interesting table, but also provides an excellent source of conversation.

Flowers add a tremendous boost. While a florist who is familiar with your needs is a necessity if you entertain frequently, growing your own violets, ivy plants, and orchids provides a very inexpensive source. A friend of ours brought us a simple basket holding a gorgeous African violet plant. We have used this beautiful centerpiece on many occasions.

Entertaining does not have to be complicated or expensive. If your taste is champagne and caviar but your budget is hot dogs and soda, instead try an American golden caviar with toast points and cream cheese served with an imported beer in champagne flutes. Add the crisply starched linen napkins that you picked up at a garage sale and Grandma's china. Voilà!

Plan the event carefully. Consider the number of people you expect and your budget. Tailor the menu to fit these figures and then estimate the amount of time that you will have for food preparation, table setting and flower arrangements. What is the parking situation? Should a valet parking company be hired? Will you need a bartender, service personnel, a cleanup crew? What will the weather be like? For a large number of people you may need a coat-check person. These are just a few of the questions you must ask yourself, not only to determine your budget, but to make sure all services required from outside the home are arranged in advance. Make a list of those providing services, with whom you spoke, on what day, telephone and/or fax numbers and follow-up required. Select dependable people. Then once the arrangements have been made, call them three days before the event to reconfirm.

Setting up your kitchen for food preparation is just as important as the menu. Organization is the key to easygoing entertainment.

Choose a menu you are comfortable with that can be prepared easily. There is no point in trying to accomplish a complicated menu that will stress you out. After all, this *is supposed* to be fun. If you are still in the shower when your guests begin to arrive, you are probably in trouble.

When entertaining during a hectic time, use already-prepared food items along with your own creations, or select items you can make a week ahead of time that freeze well. Keep in mind the limitations of your oven and refrigerator.

When it is time to begin preparing the food, take time to cross-reference recipe ingredients. Prepare enough minced garlic for all recipes that call for minced garlic. Trim and wash your produce at the same time and have it ready for assembly. Think about items requiring processing, then arrange use of the food processor so you do not need to wash the bowl in between each item. For instance, if you need to mince parsley, basil, onions, leeks and garlic, do it in that exact order. With careful scraping with a rubber spatula, you will not need to wash the bowl until finished.

Set the pace with relaxing background music. Think things through, relax and enjoy yourself knowing that the fruits of your labor will be applauded.

Harry Schwartz

*This Book is Dedicated
to
My Wife, Laurie,
My daughter, Alexa,
And my mother, Alyseann –
My Ever Flowing Sources
Of Inspiration*

*Chapter II*

# THE GREAT OUTDOORS

Entertaining outside does not always mean hamburgers and hot dogs on the grill in the backyard. Being outside opens up more than doors. It allows for the ceremony of eating creative and delicious food while celebrating the beauty and bounty of the earth.

One experiences a heavenly feeling whether savoring delicacies like grilled lobster or appreciating the simple flavors of fresh fruit, "en plein air." The Impressionist painters found inspiration and vitality in creating their masterpieces outdoors. Likewise, when preparing foods and entertaining, all of the senses come into play. The ingredients become your paints, the utensils your brushes, and the resulting masterpieces will be yours!

Combining some of the following recipes for an outdoor feast will be like an exhibition. Put together the Grilled Chicken and Lemon Sauce with some grilled vegetables, New Potato Salad, Almond Bars and a light white wine for a standing ovation.

*Chapter II*

# THE GREAT OUTDOORS
## Recipe List

Chili Fried Chicken
Guacamole Tacos
London Broil Sandwiches
Grilled Chicken with Lemon Sauce
Grilled Lobster
Lobster Rolls
Crab Cakes with Purple Peppers
English Burgers
Miami Sandwiches
Georgetown Club
Sesame Chicken Salad Sandwiches
New Potato Salad
Fried Yam Chips
Husk Grilled Sweet Corn
Grilled Vegetables
Grilled Greens
Layer Bars
Chocolate Almond Bars
Raspberries in Raspberry Iced Tea
Fresh Lemonade

# Chili Fried Chicken

Here's a Southwestern twist to a great southern classic. The chili powder used here can be either mild or hot depending on personal preferences. This method also works well for fish fillets by twisting a lemon slice over the fillet just before serving. The tangy, tingling sensation created by the addition of chili powder causes joyful anticipation of every bite!.

**12 pieces frying chicken**
**2 cups milk**
**1 cup all-purpose flour**
**2 cups coarsely crushed cornflakes**
**1 cup plain bread crumbs**
**1 tablespoon cracked pepper**
**1 tablespoon chili powder**
**1 tablespoon salt**
**4 eggs, lightly beaten**
**1 cup vegetable oil for frying**

1. Soak chicken in milk overnight.
2. Roll chicken pieces in flour.
3. Mix together cornflakes, bread crumbs, cracked pepper, chili powder, and salt.
4. Dip chicken into beaten egg and then roll in cornflake mixture.
5. Heat one-half of the oil in a large, heavy skillet over medium-high heat until it is very hot, but not smoking. Arrange 6 pieces of chicken in pan. Fry until very brown and crispy, approximately 9 minutes per side, turning once. Juices of chicken will run clear when done.
6. Drain on paper-towel-lined tray in warm oven while frying the remaining chicken in the other half of oil.

**Serves 6–8**

# Guacamole Tacos

By the pool or on the beach, these tacos make a great lunch or snack. The cool richness of the avocado, blended with cilantro and a dash of Tabasco, combined with the crispness of the warm corn taco shell, pleases the eye as well as the palate. They are best when prepared just before eating. In Mexico, to maintain the rich green color, the pit of the avocado is often placed in the center of the completed dish. A squeeze of lemon also helps to preserve the color.

**4 ripe avocados**
**½ cup chopped tomato**
**¼ cup chopped onion**
**⅛ cup minced cilantro**
**2 teaspoons fresh lemon juice**
**1 teaspoon salt**
**Dash Tabasco sauce**
**2 tablespoons mayonnaise**
**12 taco shells**
**1 cup shredded lettuce**
**1 cup chopped tomato**
**½ cup black olives, pitted drained and sliced**
**1 cup shredded cheddar cheese**

1. Mix together the avocado, tomato, onion, cilantro, lemon juice, salt, and Tabasco to combine well, then mash avocado. Frost top of mixture with mayonnaise and cover with plastic wrap. Refrigerate.
2. Warm the taco shells in an oven, on the grill, or in the sun on top of aluminum foil.
3. Stir guacamole to incorporate mayonnaise and divide among taco shells.
4. Serve with lettuce, tomato, black olives, and shredded cheddar.

**Serves 6–8**

## London Broil Sandwiches

*These make an elegant tailgate or picnic. The meal is complete served on a silver tray around a mound of new potato salad. The pineapple juice, mixed with soy and garlic, lends a sweet Oriental taste to the juicy charred meat which, when chilled and thinly sliced, will be sampled before the sandwiches are even assembled. While this recipe calls for six-inch crusty rolls, my wife and I have served this sandwich on large baguettes sliced into finger sandwiches for a buffet.*

**1 flank steak, 3 to 4 pounds**
**2 cups pineapple juice**
**¼ cup soy sauce**
**1 tablespoon minced garlic**
**3 tablespoons mayonnaise**
**1 tablespoon Dijon mustard**
**8 radicchio leaves, rinsed and patted dry**
**8 6-inch crusty rolls**

1. Place flank steak in rectangular 11"x7"x2" glass dish. Mix together the juice, soy sauce, and garlic and pour over meat. Cover and refrigerate up to 48 hours.
2. Grill meat over hot coals for 4 minutes per side for medium rare meat.
3. Remove from heat and allow to stand for 15 minutes before slicing thinly across the grain of the meat.
4. Split rolls and spread mustard and mayonnaise on tops and bottoms. Divide meat among roll bottoms, top with radicchio and roll tops.

**Yields: 8 sandwiches**
**Serves 4**

# Grilled Chicken With Lemon Sauce

This is a novel way to serve chicken, since most people are used to the traditional Oriental-style lemon chicken. This skinless grilled version is much lighter (and less fattening), and the citrus brings out its wonderful flavor. Sweet and tangy with a robust garlic flavor, this chicken is a definite hit.

- 1 cup soy sauce
- 1 cup orange juice
- ⅛ cup safflower oil
- 2 tablespoons fresh ginger, peeled and minced
- 2 tablespoons fresh cracked pepper
- 4 chicken breasts, cut in half, skinned and boned
- 2 cups granulated sugar
- ¼ cup water
- 1 tablespoon minced garlic
- ⅛ cup grated lemon zest
- 3 cups chow mein noodles

1. Mix together soy sauce, orange juice, safflower oil, ginger, and cracked pepper. Pour over chicken. Cover and marinate in refrigerator for up to 24 hours.
2. Grill chicken over hot coals about 4 minutes on each side or until juices run clear. Remove from grill and allow to stand for 10 minutes.
3. Slice chicken across grain. Cover in glass dish with juices and keep warm in oven.
4. Place sugar and water in heavy sauce pan over medium high heat. When mixture begins to bubble, reduce heat to keep softly bubbling for 15 minutes. Turn off heat and stir in garlic and lemon zest.
5. Place chicken over chow mein noodles and pour sauce over top. Serve immediately.

**Serves 6–8**

# Grilled Lobster

A favorite of ours when in Maine, since lobster is so delicious and inexpensive, we always make enough for leftovers. The sweet meat with the grilled flavor can be chopped and mixed with jack cheese, folded into a tortilla and grilled for a fabulous lobster quesadilla.

**6–8 1¼-pound live Maine lobsters**
**A large pot of salted boiling water**
**½ cup lightly salted butter**
**1 teaspoon minced garlic**

1. In batches of two or three, plunge the lobsters into the boiling water to kill. This will also cause them to "purge" the contents of their intestines. After 2 minutes, remove the lobsters from the boiling water and run them under cold water to stop the cooking process. Repeat with all lobsters.

2. With a sharp knife, split the lobsters in two down the middle, following the line down the back and tail. Remove lobster innards and veins.

3. Melt butter with garlic and baste tail meat. Place lobsters, meat side up, over hot coals for 4 minutes. Baste again and turn lobsters over. Grill 4 minutes more or until lobster meat just turns from pink to white.

**Serves 6–8**

# *Lobster Rolls*

Here's one of the first lunch experiences many people have when visiting coastal Maine. The lobster is so fresh and delicious it is almost impossible to tire of this treat. Preparing this at home is a bit of a mess but well worth the effort.

- 3 1½-pound live lobsters
- ½ cup mayonnaise
- 1 teaspoon fresh lemon juice
- ⅛ cup minced sweet gherkins
- 1 teaspoon prepared mustard
- 8 hard-crusted rolls

1. Bring a large pot of salted water to a raging boil. Drop in lobsters and cover. Boil for 12 minutes. Turn off heat and let stand 3 minutes.
2. Take lobsters from pot and rinse in cold water. Remove lobster meat from shells, rinse, pat dry, and cut into chunks.
3. Mix together mayonnaise, lemon juice, gherkins, and mustard. Toss lobster with dressing and divide among split crusty rolls.

**Serves 6–8**

# Crab Cakes With Purple Peppers

*Florida crabmeat is so easy to find on the Treasure Coast of Florida. Crabmeat from a tin will work well for these crab cakes but fresh is always preferred. Because of the addition of yellow corn and chunks of purple pepper (red bell pepper will work as well), when fried to a crisp golden brown on the outside these are most attractive and delicious. While ocktail sauce or tartar sauce are common garnishes, try chopping a tomato and tossing with a little minced garlic, some cracked pepper, olive oil, and a pinch of salt for a great combination of flavor and color.*

- 1 pound fresh boiled crab meat, picked over for shell, rinsed and drained
- 1 cup yellow corn kernels, frozen or vacuum packed, rinsed and drained
- ½ cup diced purple bell pepper,[*] trimmed and seeded
- 1 teaspoon lemon juice
- 2 teaspoons salt
- 1 tablespoon cracked pepper
- 3 eggs, lightly beaten
- 2 tablespoons ketchup
- dash Tabasco sauce
- 1 to 2 cups breadcrumbs
- ¼ cup butter or margarine for frying

1. Mix together crab, corn, purple bell pepper, lemon juice, salt, and pepper. Fold in eggs, ketchup, and Tabasco. Stir in 1 cup breadcrumbs, or more as needed to form patties.
2. Mold 3-inch to 4-inch patties and place on tray lined with waxed paper dusted with breadcrumbs. Sprinkle tops of patties with breadcrumbs.

*Continued*

---

[*] Bell peppers are mild, sweet and most juicy peppers. They are named because of their shape being similar to a bell.

3. Heat butter or margarine in large, heavy sauté pan over medium-high heat. Arrange cakes in pan and fry for 5 minutes. Reduce heat to medium and when cakes are golden brown, turn to cook and brown other side, about 10 minutes more.

*Yields: 16 crab cakes*
*Serves 6–8*

**NOTES**

# English Burgers

*These are really flavorful burgers — certainly a cut above the norm. The fried egg is optional, but such a valuable addition to this combination. These can be made as part of a spectacular Sunday brunch.*

- 2 pounds ground sirloin
- 1 cup chopped red onion
- 3 eggs, slightly beaten
- 1 tablespoon Worcestershire sauce
- 1 teaspoon salt
- 2 tablespoons cracked pepper
- 8 English muffins, split, buttered, and broiled until browned
- 8 cheddar cheese slices
- 8 tomato slices
- 16 slices crisp bacon
- 8 eggs, fried over easy in butter, or margarine

1. Mix together the beef, onion, eggs, Worcestershire, salt, and pepper. Form 8 patties slightly larger in diameter than the muffins. Grill patties about 4 minutes on each side or until cooked to preference.
2. Assemble burgers by stacking muffin bottom, then burger, cheese, tomato, bacon and fried egg. Top with muffin top and serve.

**Yields: 8 burgers**

## Miami Sandwiches

Miami is as famous for its high population of Jewish people as New York. As Jews go, so go the delicatessens. The Rascal House has been around since before I was born and there are still lines of people waiting to be seated at any hour of the day and night. These sandwiches create an elegant statement and can be enjoyed in the comfort of your own home. They are also terrific on a picnic or tailgate with cole slaw or a simple salad. A dry Champagne completes the picture.

**8 ounces cream cheese, softened**
**¼ cup chopped scallions**
**¼ cup pitted and chopped black olives**
**8 bagels, split, buttered, and broiled until browned**
**8 thin slices tomato**
**1 pound smoked salmon,[*] thinly sliced**
**8 radicchio leaves, rinsed and patted dry**

1. Mix together the cream cheese, scallion, and olives. Spread on toasted bagel bottoms.
2. Place a slice of tomato on each bagel bottom. Roll salmon pieces and divide among sandwiches. Top with radicchio and bagel top or serve open-faced.

**Yields: 8 sandwiches**

---

[*] Nova or smoked salmon work well.

# Georgetown Club

*I came up with this combination during a summer at George Washington University, in Washington, D.C. What a town — so much to eat and so little time! This combination is deliciously colorful and contains the ingredients of an entire meal.*

- 3 cups white meat chicken or turkey, cooked and diced
- ¼ cup chopped sweet gherkins
- ¾ cup mayonnaise
- 16 slices egg bread, toasted and lightly buttered
- 16 slices crisp, lean bacon
- 16 avocado slices (about 3 avocados)
- 8 slices tomato
- 1 cup shredded mixed salad greens
- 8 slices Havarti[*] cheese

1. Mix together chicken or turkey, gherkins, and mayonnaise. Divide among 8 slices of toast, buttered side up.
2. Top each with 2 slices bacon, 2 slices avocado, a tomato slice, some shredded greens and a slice of cheese. Put slice of toast, buttered side down on each, cut in half and serve.

**Yields: 8 sandwiches**

---

[*] Or substitute any mild, tangy semisoft cheese.

# Sesame Chicken Sandwiches

*These sandwiches are superb for chicken leftovers. They can be assembled just before serving with the chicken having been prepared up to 36 hours in advance. Blending sesame, scallions and peanut butter with the hoisin sauce creates a color and taste that is characteristic of Thailand.*

**4 chicken breasts, skinless and boneless, cut in halves**
**1 cup soy sauce**
**1 tablespoon safflower oil, or other light oil**
**¾ cup sesame seeds**
**½ cup chopped scallions**
**¼ cup mayonnaise**
**¼ cup hoisin sauce***
**¼ cup creamy peanut butter**
**1 tablespoon sesame oil**
**16 slices pumpernickel bread**
**1 cup shredded salad greens**

1. Mix together soy and oil. Marinate chicken with soy sauce and safflower oil up to 36 hours. Grill over hot coals for 5 minutes on each side or until juices run clear. Remove, cool, wrap in plastic wrap, and refrigerate.
2. Place sesame seeds in skillet over medium-high heat and toast until brown. Cool.
3. Mix together the sesame seeds, scallions, mayonnaise, hoisin, peanut butter, and sesame oil.
4. Cut up the chicken into small chunks and toss with dressing. Divide among 8 slices of bread and top with some shredded greens and the other slice of bread.

**Yields: 8 sandwiches**

---

*Available at Oriental supermarkets or the import section of a supermarket.

# New Potato Salad

There are myriad ways to make potato salad, but this one brings in the most compliments. With grilled meats and fish or almost any sandwich, you cannot go wrong. This one is light and has great texture, combining the crunch of sweet gherkins with the tang of dill.

5 pounds small new potatoes, scrubbed, peeled, and boiled until tender
2 cups mayonnaise
¼ cup prepared mustard
1 cup onion, minced
½ cup minced sweet gherkins
1 tablespoon celery seed
1 tablespoon dried dill weed
4 eggs, hard-boiled and chopped

1. Quarter the potatoes and toss in a bowl with the balance of ingredients to mix well. Cover with plastic wrap directly on top of salad. Refrigerate overnight if possible.

**Serves 6–8**

# *Fried Yam Chips*

These are really a treat and so good with sandwiches. They are super with beer. too. Yams — truly a gift of the gods. Typically grown in Latin America, yams are not the same thing as sweet potatoes, though they are often interchanged because of their similar flavor. When choosing yams, look for firm and non-wrinkled skin and keep in mind that the darker the color, the sweeter the flavor.

> **2 cups yams or sweet potatoes, scrubbed, peeled and sliced thin with vegetable peeler**
> **2 cups vegetable oil, or enough for 3 inches in bottom of pot**
> **1 tablespoon salt, or to taste**

1. Heat oil in heavy, deep pot or kettle until very hot, but not smoking. Fry yam slices in batches until crisp and remove to paper towel-lined tray held in warm oven. Sprinkle with salt and serve immediately.

**Serves 6–8**

# Husk Grilled Sweet Corn

This is an entertaining way to make corn for a barbecue. Steaming it ahead and grilling just before serving retains the moisture and robust flavor of the precious kernels. Have plenty of melted butter on hand!

**8 ears corn, unshucked**
**½ cup melted butter or margarine**

1. Place corn in hot steamer and steam for 20 to 30 minutes or until corn is tender but firm. Leave as much room as possible between the ears of corn for even steaming. Cool until comfortable to handle, then remove hairy filaments from the corn while leaving the husk intact.

2. When ready to grill corn, bring to room temperature and grill over very warm, but not red, coals for 3 minutes on each side. Pull back husks and serve.

**Serves 6-8**

## Grilled Vegetables

With this fabulous and relatively low-fat way to prepare vegetables, you can make your entire meal on the grill for easy cleanup.

**Assorted vegetables:**
- 4 baking potatoes sliced into ¼-inch slices
- 2 onions sliced into 4 thick slices each
- 4 leeks split in half lengthwise
- 4 yams or sweet potatoes sliced into ¼-inch slices
- 4 small zucchini split in half lengthwise
- 2 eggplants sliced into ½-inch rounds
- 4 steamed artichokes split in half lengthwise, choke removed
- 3 heads elephant garlic

**For each vegetable:**
- ⅛ cup safflower oil
- salt and pepper to taste

1. Place vegetable, oil, salt and pepper in zipper-lock plastic bag and shake to coat. Drain off any excess oil.
2. Grill over medium-hot coals, turning once, until tender when poked with the tip of a sharp knife, about 5 minutes per side, depending on vegetable.

**Serves 6–8**

# Grilled Greens

*Topped with crumbled goat or bleu cheese, this becomes a very different way to serve a salad. It is also a light complement to a supper of grilled meat or fish.*

**Assorted vegetables:**
- 4 heads Belgian endive
- 4 heads Romaine lettuce
- 4 heads Boston or bibb lettuce
- 4 heads radicchio

- ¼ cup olive oil
- 1 tablespoon cracked pepper
- 1 tablespoon salt
- 1 teaspoon minced garlic

1. Mix together oil, salt, pepper, and garlic.
2. Cut heads of greens in half through the cores to keep leaves intact. Wash thoroughly and trim as needed.
3. Paint cut sides with oil and grill over hot coals for 60 seconds, or until core is tender but leaves are not brown. Serve immediately.

**Serves 6–8**

# Layer Bars

*These are so simple to make. They melt in your mouth and when cut for serving, look lovely as the rich layers reveal themselves. They freeze beautifully and last four or five days when kept airtight.*

**½ cup butter**
**1 cup graham cracker crumbs**
**1 12-ounce bag semisweet chocolate chips**
**1 cup chopped pecans**
**1 12-ounce bag butterscotch chips**
**1 7-ounce bag shredded coconut**
**1 14-ounce can sweetened condensed milk**

1. Melt butter in an ovenproof 8" x 12" glass baking dish by placing dish in preheated 350-degree F. oven just until butter is melted. Remove from oven.
2. Sprinkle the graham cracker crumbs in an even layer over butter, then sprinkle chocolate chips in an even layer over the graham cracker crumbs.
3. In even layers, sprinkle nuts, then butterscotch chips, then coconut, and finally pour sweetened condensed milk in a smooth layer over all.
4. Bake in 350-degree F. oven for 55 minutes or until top is golden brown. Allow to cool thoroughly before cutting.

**Yields: 24 bars**

# Chocolate Almond Bars

*These remind me of Almond Joy candy bars. They enhance any picnic or gathering.*

> ½ cup butter
> 1 cup crushed chocolate wafer cookies
> 12 ounces semisweet chocolate chips
> 1 cup slivered almonds
> 7 ounces shredded coconut
> 1 7-ounce can sweetened condensed milk

1. In ovenproof 8" x 12" glass baking dish, melt butter by placing dish in preheated 350-degree F. oven just until butter is melted. Remove from oven.
2. Sprinkle cookie crumbs in an even layer over butter.
3. In even layers, sprinkle chocolate chips, then almonds, then coconut. Finally pour sweetened condensed milk in a smooth layer over the top.
4. Bake in 350-degree F. oven for 45 minutes or until top is golden brown. Allow to cool thoroughly before cutting.

**Yields: 24 bars**

# Raspberries In Raspberry Iced Tea

*Try this for a luncheon or afternoon tea by the pool. Delicious tasting and a wonderful presentation.*

> 1 cup granulated sugar
> ½ cup water
> 1 cup fresh raspberries
> 2 quarts fresh raspberry tea,* room temperature

1. Place sugar and water in heavy saucepan over medium-high heat. When mixture begins to bubble, reduce heat to medium-low and simmer for 10 minutes. Turn off heat and stir in raspberries. Cool.
2. Spoon mixture into ice cube trays and freeze.
3. Place frozen raspberry cubes in tall glasses and pour in tea.

**Yields: About 8 glasses of tea**

---

* Available at most supermarkets.

# Fresh Lemonade

*So refreshing and easy to prepare, this should be served often in the summer.*

**Ice Cubes:**
1½ cups granulated sugar
½ cup water
24 maraschino cherries without stems, drained

**Lemonade:**
¼ cup lemon juice
2 quarts water
1 cup granulated sugar

1. **To make cubes:** Heat the sugar and water in heavy saucepan over medium-high heat until mixture begins to bubble. Reduce heat to medium-low and simmer 10 minutes.
2. Cool and pour into ice cube trays. Place a cherry in each compartment and place in freezer until frozen.
3. **To serve lemonade:** Mix together lemon juice, water, and sugar. Place ice cubes in tall glasses and pour in lemonade.

**Yields: About 8 glasses**

*Chapter III*

# ELEGANT, EASY AND LIGHT

When deciding what to serve for an event, it is important to consider many factors in order to create a great dining experience.

First, consider to whom the food will be served. Older people tend to eat less and often prefer less spicy foods and little garlic. Fish and chicken are a safe bet since meat has been crossed off many lists because of fat content and difficulty in digesting. If vegetarians are present, find out their diet preferences or health restrictions.

Season and time of day should also be considered. A hearty beef stew on a 90-degree summer day will not sit well. Likewise, an entrée salad may not fill up your guests on a cold day. A rich meal is often more appropriate in the evening than for lunch. In sum, common sense comes into light when planning any menu.

Think about what will be happening during or after the event. Will people want to dance after a heavy meal? Will they like doubles tennis after that lasagna?

Finally, consider budget and the availability of ingredients. Is flying in fresh California figs in my budget? Are lobsters in season? NEVER use frozen stone crab claws and never consume mussels or clams in a month without an "r" in its name. Use ingredients in season to maximize value and flavor. It will make the day a better one!

*Chapter III*

# ELEGANT, EASY AND LIGHT
## Recipe List

*Bruschetta*
*Toasted Goat Cheese Salad*
*Italian Style Chicken Livers*
*Olive Sauté*
*Lemon Shrimp in Grape Leaves*
*Scallops in the Shell*

*Stuffed Eggplant*
*Spinach Stuffed Potatoes*
*Basic Blintzes*
*Herbed Cheese Blintzes*
*Artichoke Tart*
*Mediterranean Salad*
*Marinated Artichokes with Mushrooms*
*Zucchini and Porcini*
*Garlic Parmesan Vinaigrette*
*Bacon Gorgonzola Vinaigrette*
*Garlic Garbanzo Vinaigrette*
*Honey Lemon Dressing*
*Eggless Caesar Dressing*
*Italian Salad*

Continued

*Tabbouleh Pepper Salad*
*Cauliflower Salad*
*Tuna Pignolia Salad*
*Indian Tuna Salad*
*Gingered Carrots*
*Endive and Lupini Bean Salad*
*Vegetable Sandwiches*
*Cucumber Tea Sandwiches*
*Cheddar Pea Salad*
*Caramelized Potatoes*
*Cheesy Spinach*
*Chicken Salad Louisiana*
*Twice Baked Potatoes*
*Swiss Cheese Potatoes*
*Chocolate Caramel Fondue*
*Phyllo Pastry with Feta and Spinach*
*Basic Quiche with Variations*
*Blackened Chicken Breasts*
*Veal with artichokes and Capers*
*Red Veal with Scallops*
*Poulet Suisse*
*Veal with Prosciutto*

# *Bruschetta*

Here's an easy and delectable appetizer that seems to please just about everyone. It's fresh tasting and low in fat, and can be served atop shredded greens with crostini on the side. Always use fresh basil. Prepare the ingredients in advance and combine just before serving. Crostini make excellent croutons.

## Topping

- 2 cups diced firm ripe tomatoes
- 1 tablespoon minced fresh garlic
- ½ cup minced fresh basil
- ¼ cup minced fresh parsley
- 1 tablespoon granulated sugar
- 1 teaspoon salt
- 1 teaspoon cracked black pepper
- ¼ cup olive oil

## Crostini

- 1 loaf French bread, baguette size, cut into 18 1-inch slices
- 4 ounces butter or margarine
- 1 tablespoon minced garlic

1. Place topping ingredients in glass bowl and toss gently to mix, being careful not to crush the tomatoes.

2. Make crostini by heating butter and garlic in large sauté pan until garlic begins to brown. Arrange bread slices in pan in batches and fry on both sides until golden brown and toasted. Keep loosely wrapped in foil in 200-degree F. oven until ready to assemble bruschetta.

**Serves 6–8**

# *Toasted Goat Cheese Salad*

*This salad always gets raves. It is a perfect lunch or light supper when served with homemade bread and a bottle of wine. For a heartier meal, arrange sliced smoked chicken or beef around the goat cheese. Some types of fresh goat cheese can be molded into patties while other types must be cut. The toasted goat cheese, when served alongside crackers or crostini, makes a delectable appetizer.*

## Toasted Goat Cheese

- 1 cup plain breadcrumbs
- 1 tablespoon dried oregano
- 1 tablespoon dried basil
- 1 tablespoon cracked black pepper
- 1 teaspoon salt
- 1 pound fresh goat cheese cut or molded into 6 patties*
- 2 eggs, slightly beaten in small shallow bowl for dipping patties
- 4 ounces butter or margarine
- 1 teaspoon minced garlic

## Dressing

- 1 tablespoon minced garlic
- 1 teaspoon salt
- 1 teaspoon cracked pepper
- 1 tablespoon granulated sugar
- 1 tablespoon fresh minced or 1 teaspoon dried oregano
- ¼ cup red wine vinegar
- ½ cup olive oil

*Continued*

---

\* To cut logs of goat cheese, use a piece of thread or unwaxed dental floss held tightly wrapped around both index fingers.

## Salad
**6 cups coarsely shredded fresh salad greens**

1. Mix together breadcrumbs, oregano, basil, pepper, and salt in a shallow dish. Dip goat cheese patty into beaten eggs and dredge in breadcrumb mixture to coat thoroughly. Set on waxed paper until all are complete.
2. Heat butter in large nonstick sauté pan over medium-high heat and add garlic. Arrange patties in pan and fry for about 5 minutes or until golden brown on bottom. Carefully turn and reduce heat to medium for 5 more minutes, then turn off heat.
3. Mix together dressing ingredients and toss with salad greens. Divide among 6 plates and top each salad with toasted goat cheese patty. Serve immediately.

**Serves 6**

# Italian Style Chicken Livers

*This is a perfect Sunday evening supper accompanied by crusty bread and a bottle of Chianti. The combination of oregano, basil and garlic with the tartness of sun-dried tomatoes is tantalizing. The richness of the livers and wine makes this a most savory dish. Served without the pasta in a chafing dish, they're a marvelous cocktail buffet entree. For a fabulous first course, serve on top of crostini.*

- ½ cup all-purpose flour
- 1 teaspoon salt
- 1 teaspoon cracked pepper
- 2 pounds fresh chicken livers, rinsed and drained
- ¼ cup safflower oil, or other light oil
- 4 ounces butter or margarine
- 2 tablespoons minced fresh garlic
- 1 cup chopped onion
- 1 cup chopped red pepper
- ½ cup chopped celery
- ¼ cup chopped fresh basil
- ¼ cup chopped fresh parsley
- 1 tablespoon minced fresh oregano, or 1 teaspoon dried
- 1 cup minced sun-dried tomatoes
- 1 cup dry white wine
- 1 pound dried, or 2 pounds fresh, angel hair pasta
- 1 tablespoon olive oil
- Grated Parmesan cheese

1. Place flour, salt, and pepper into zipper-lock plastic bag, capturing some air while sealing bag. Shake to mix contents. Add chicken livers and shake to coat thoroughly.

2. Heat oil in large sauté pan over medium-high heat until very hot. Test this with a small piece of bread which should brown in about 30 seconds.

*Continued*

3. Carefully arrange livers in hot oil with tongs, being careful not to get spattered. Sauté about 5 minutes on each side until exteriors are browned and slightly crusty. Remove to drain on paper-towel-lined tray and place in 200-degree F. oven.

4. Drain any excess oil from sauté pan and return pan to medium-high heat. Heat butter until it has stopped bubbling. Add garlic, onion, red pepper, celery, basil, parsley, oregano, and dried tomatoes to pan and sauté for 5 minutes or until vegetables begin to get tender. Stir in wine and simmer for 5 more minutes. Turn off heat.

5. Cook pasta according to directions. Drain and toss with olive oil. Set aside.

6. Turn on heat under sauté pan to medium-high, and when mixture boils, gently stir in chicken livers. Remove from heat.

7. Form pasta into nests on hot serving plates and divide chicken liver mixture among nests. Serve immediately with grated Parmesan cheese.

**Serves 6**

# Olive Sauté

This is marvelous as a side dish, atop a grilled steak, or simply tossed with some fresh cooked pasta. The salt from the olives and the tang from the scallions and garlic simply work wonders. It also makes a delicious sandwich when placed between a slices of crusty French bread with ripe Brie cheese.

> 2 tablespoons olive oil
> 1 tablespoon minced fresh garlic
> 1 pound Greek olives, pitted and halved
> 1 pound green olives,* pitted and halved
> 1 cup chopped scallions
> 1 cup sliced cucumber, peeled and seeded
> Juice of 1 lemon
> 2 tablespoons chopped fresh basil, or 2 teaspoons dried
> 1 tablespoon minced fresh oregano, or 1 teaspoon dried
> 1 tablespoon cracked pepper

1. Heat oil in large sauté pan over medium-high heat. Add garlic and cook until garlic begins to brown. Stir in remaining ingredients and sauté 5 to 6 minutes. Serve immediately.

**Serves 6 as a side or pasta dish**

---

\* Use pimiento stuffed olives. Pimiento adds great color.

# Lemon Shrimp In Grape Leaves

*These delicate morsels make a refreshing poolside supper on a warm summer evening. They are superb as an accent addition to any buffet or served to guests as a first course. The hint of licorice from the ouzo gives this dish a kick. The fresh, lemony yogurt sauce makes it a Middle Eastern star.*

## Shrimp

- 2 tablespoons olive oil
- 1 tablespoon minced garlic
- 1 pound uncooked shrimp, peeled, deveined, cut into bite sized pieces, and patted dry
- 1 teaspoon dried Greek oregano,* or 1 tablespoon dried regular oregano
- 1 teaspoon salt
- 1 teaspoon cracked pepper
- 1 cup ouzo**
- 2 cups cooked glutinous rice, as for sushi
- 18 brine-cured grape leaves***, rinsed and patted dry
- 2 eggs, lightly beaten in shallow dish with room to dip stuffed leaves
- 1 cup breadcrumbs for coating
- 4 ounces butter, or margarine

## Yogurt Sauce

- 1 cup plain yogurt
- Juice of 1 lemon
- ½ cup chopped cucumber, peeled and seeded
- 1 teaspoon paprika

**Continued**

---

\* Available at specialty markets.

\*\* A clear, anise-flavored liqueur available at most liquor stores.

\*\*\* Available at most Mediterranean food stores or gourmet markets.

*Elegant, Easy and Light*

1. Heat oil in large sauté pan over medium-high heat. Add garlic and sauté until it begins to brown. Add shrimp, oregano, salt, and pepper and sauté about 90 seconds. Add ouzo and reduce heat to medium. Stir in rice, mix thoroughly, and set aside to cool.
2. Spoon mixture in a small mound onto grape leaves near the bottom of each leaf. Fold bottom of leaf over filling, bring sides of leaf to middle over bottom flap, and roll up leaf, resulting in a round blintz-type shape.
3. Dip each stuffed leaf into egg and coat with breadcrumbs. Set aside on waxed paper.
4. Heat butter in large sauté pan over medium-high heat and brown each stuffed leaf on two sides. This can be done in batches. The finished leaves can be held on an ovenproof serving platter in a 200-degree F. oven.
5. Mix together sauce ingredients and refrigerate until ready to serve.
6. Serve stuffed leaves warm with sauce on the side.

**Serves 6**

# Scallops In The Shell

This is an attractive dish for lunch or a light supper. It is a dramatic presentation and requires a little extra effort, but the shells can be made up two days ahead of time, kept tightly wrapped, and heated in the oven before assembling. If the shells have been frozen, bring them to room temperature before assembling.

I find bay scallops to be sweeter than sea scallops and their size is, or course, much smaller. Either will work for this recipe, but I much prefer bay scallops. The unusual thing about this scallop dish is that you can eat the shell!

- 6 pastry scallop shells (recipe follows)
- 4 ounces butter or margarine
- 1 teaspoon minced fresh garlic
- ⅔ cup finely sliced leeks
- 1 pound sliced white mushrooms
- 1 pound fresh bay scallops (or 1 pound sea scallops, quartered)
- ⅛ cup chopped fresh basil
- 1 tablespoon salt
- 1 teaspoon cracked pepper
- ½ teaspoon ground nutmeg (optional)
- 1 teaspoon paprika
- 2 tablespoons all-purpose flour
- ¼ cup cognac
- ¾ cup cream or whole milk
- ½ cup grated Parmesan cheese

## Shells

This makes enough for 12 shells or 6 shells and 1 pie crust bottom.

- 1¾ cup unbleached, all-purpose flour
- 1 teaspoon salt
- 1⅓ cup unsalted butter, chilled and diced
- ⅓ cup vegetable shortening, chilled and divided into pieces
- ¼ to ⅓ cup very cold water

*Continued*

## Shells

1. Place flour and salt into food processor with metal blade.
2. Add butter and shortening and pulse until contents resemble a coarse meal.
3. Process while adding water in a slow stream until mixture begins to gather around blade into a ball.
4. Turn out contents onto floured surface, knead for a quick 30 seconds, and roll into ball. Wrap tightly and refrigerate for 30 minutes.
5. Heat oven to 375 degrees F. Roll out dough to approximately ¼-inch thickness.
6. To make 12 shells, cut pieces of dough generously, sized around washed and dried scallop shells. Tightly wrap 24 scallop shells in aluminum foil and place each sized piece of dough between two wrapped shells. Press together firmly. Repeat with all shells. Bake in oven about 25 minutes or until shells begin to brown and puff up.
7. Remove top foil-wrapped shells and bake 5 minutes more. Remove pastry shells to rack to cool.

## Scallop Filling

1. Heat butter in pan over medium-high heat until foam subsides. Add garlic, leeks, and mushrooms and sauté for 5 minutes. Add scallops, basil, salt, pepper, nutmeg, and paprika and sauté for 90 seconds. Sprinkle flour over mixture, stir for 30 seconds and then pour in cognac. Stir and slowly add cream or milk. Reduce heat to medium-low and stir for about 2 minutes while mixture thickens.
2. Divide mixture among 6 shells and top each with one-sixth of the cheese. Place on low shelf under broiler until tops are brown. Serve immediately.

*Serves 6*

# Stuffed Eggplant

*This dish is similar to cannelloni, with eggplant standing in for the pasta. It is a wise choice when entertaining vegetarian friends, many of whom are served pasta on a regular basis. The tomato sauce is almost like a warm tomato chutney. It's divine.*

## Eggplant Shells

- 2 cups plain breadcrumbs
- 2 tablespoons salt
- 2 tablespoons cracked pepper
- 2–3 eggplants, sliced lengthwise into 12 ½-inch thick slices
- 3 eggs, slightly beaten in flat dish large enough to dip eggplant
- 2 tablespoons olive oil
- 1 tablespoon minced fresh garlic

1. Mix together breadcrumbs, salt, and pepper. Dip each slice of eggplant into egg and then dredge in breadcrumbs to coat. Set aside on waxed paper.
2. Heat oil in large sauté pan over medium-high heat and add garlic. Sauté garlic until it begins to brown. Fry eggplant slices in batches until browned on both sides, very pliable and somewhat soft, about 6 minutes on each side. Remove to waxed paper.

## Stuffing

- 1 pound fresh ricotta cheese
- ½ cup fresh basil, trimmed and chopped
- ¼ cup parsley, trimmed and chopped
- ¼ cup scallion, trimmed and chopped
- ½ cup grated Parmesan cheese

1. Combine all filling ingredients and beat with a fork for about 1 minute to fluff.

*Continued*

2. Place a dollop of the filling on the bottom of each slice of eggplant and roll up each piece. Wooden toothpicks may be used to fasten, but with a little care and the aid of a flat spatula this can be avoided. Arrange rolls on baking dish.

## Sauce

    3 tablespoons olive oil
    1 tablespoon minced garlic
    ½ cup minced onion
    4 ounces tomato paste
    ¼ cup chopped fresh basil
    2 tablespoons minced fresh oregano, or 2 teaspoons dried
    2 cups coarsely chopped tomatoes, seeded
    ¾ cup dry red wine
    ⅛ cup granulated sugar
    1 cup shredded Mozzarella for browning on top

1. Heat oil in saucepan over medium-high heat. Add garlic and onion and stir about 5 minutes or until onion is soft and starts to turn golden. Reduce heat to medium and stir in tomato paste, basil, oregano and tomato.
2. Return heat to medium-high and slowly stir in wine. Reduce heat to medium when mixture begins to bubble, and sprinkle sugar on top. Stir to mix. Remove from heat.

## To complete the dish

1. Pour warm sauce over eggplant and top with shredded Mozzarella cheese. Place in oven on highest setting until cheese bubbles and begins to brown, about 7 minutes. Serve immediately.

**Serves 6**

# Spinach Stuffed Potatoes

*Spinach plus potatoes plus cheese equals success! Cooked shrimp, lobster, or crab may be added after the spinach for an even more formidable meal. Make up to 24 hours in advance and place in the oven for the final baking.*

**3 large, unblemished baking potatoes, relatively equal in size**
**4 ounces butter or margarine**
**8 ounces sour cream or crème fraîche**
**1 cup shredded mild cheddar cheese**
**1 tablespoon salt**
**1 tablespoon cracked pepper**
**3 eggs, slightly beaten**
**1 pound frozen chopped spinach, thawed and wrung-out in a towel**

1. Preheat oven to 325 degrees F. Pierce potatoes with a fork, once on each side, and place in oven to bake until tender and the skins are crisp, about 1 hour and 45 minutes.
2. Place butter in a large glass bowl. Slice hot potatoes in half by holding with a mitt and using a large, very sharp knife. Be careful not to tear the skins. Gently scoop out potato from skins onto butter in bowl to melt butter. Stir to mix.
3. Using an electric hand mixer, whip the sour cream, cheese, salt, pepper, and eggs into the potato until light and fluffy. Fold in spinach with a spatula. Divide mixture among potato skin halves. Bake stuffed potatoes in 350-degree F. oven for 30 minutes. Tops should begin to brown.

**Serves 6**

# Basic Blintzes

The blintz world is a world of discovery, one rarely explored to the fullest. Blintzes can be appetizers, entrees or desserts. Fill with chopped cooked meats, an array of cheese stuffings, or countless fruit combinations. Make in advance, storing each one between two pieces of waxed paper, with batches placed in a zipper-lock plastic bag to be used as desired. Kids love the shells lightly salted or spread with jam and rolled up.

> 3 eggs plus 1 egg yolk
> 1¼ cups whole milk
> 1 cup unbleached all-purpose flour
> 1 teaspoon salt
> 4 ounces butter or margarine for frying

1. With a whisk or fork, combine eggs, yolk, and milk in a deep bowl. Gradually stir in flour, mixing enough to combine well but leaving a few small lumps. Stir in salt.

2. Heat 1 teaspoon of butter in an 8-inch or 9-inch nonstick sauté or omelette pan over medium-high heat until the foam subsides and butter begins to turn golden. Using a ladle, place enough batter in the hot pan to cover the bottom of the pan. Swirl the pan to coat it well and evenly, then pour excess batter from pan back into bowl. Cook blintz until it begins to brown on the bottom and the edges pull away from the pan, about 2 minutes.

3. Remove blintz to kitchen towel by inverting pan and tapping it on towel-covered surface. Repeat with balance of batter, adding butter to the pan as needed for flavor and to prevent sticking.

**Yields: About 36 pancakes**

# Herbed Cheese Blintzes

*Here's an all-around favorite. Blintzes assembled in advance and then refrigerated until they are ready to be cooked are perfect for these fast-paced times.*

**1 pound ricotta cheese**
**½ cup grated Pecorino Romano cheese**
**¼ cup chopped fresh basil**
**⅛ cup chopped fresh parsley**
**1 teaspoon dried oregano**
**½ cup chopped scallions**
**1 tablespoon cracked pepper**
**12 blintz pancakes**
**2 ounces butter for frying**

1. Mix together cheeses, herbs, scallion, and pepper.
2. Using the pancakes browned side up, place a dollop of filling toward the bottom of each pancake, leaving enough pancake on the bottom to fold over filling. After folding bottom, bring sides to meet in the center and fold blintz up to enclose filling.
3. Heat butter in a large, nonstick sauté pan over medium-high heat until foam subsides. Arrange blintzes in pan in such a way that turning them over will not be a problem.
4. Fry first on the side with edges to seal blintz before turning. Carefully turn after about 5 minutes and blintzes have begun to brown. Reduce heat and fry 8 minutes over medium-low heat to brown other side. Serve immediately.

**Serves 6**

# Artichoke Tart

This is a versatile tart that can be served as a perfect lunch or light supper. It can also be made in a rectangular tart pan with a false bottom, cut into 3-inch squares and served as an appetizer or passed during cocktails. Enjoy the delicacy of the artichoke when combined with the magnificence of the imported Parmesan.

- **1 tart shell as for *Scallops in the Shell* (see page 39)**
- **5 eggs**
- **1 cup heavy cream or whole milk**
- **1 tablespoon cracked pepper**
- **1 teaspoon salt**
- **2 12-ounce jars marinated artichoke hearts, drained and patted dry**
- **1 cup fresh, whole milk Mozzarella cheese, cut into small chunks**
- **½ cup grated imported Parmesan cheese**
- **2 ounces butter, melted**

1. Preheat oven to 350 degrees F. Roll out pastry into ¼-inch sheet and roll around rolling pin. Unroll pastry over 12-inch false-bottomed tart pan, press into bottom and sides, and trim top. Crimp edges by pinching with fingers.
2. Beat together eggs, cream, pepper, and salt in a glass bowl with a pouring spout. Pour ½ cup of mixture into tart shell to coat bottom.
3. Arrange artichoke hearts and mozzarella cheese in pastry. Gently pour remaining egg mixture over artichokes and cheese. Sprinkle Parmesan over top and drizzle melted butter over Parmesan.
4. Place on foil on oven rack in lower third of oven and bake until browned and delicious, about 50 minutes. Remove from oven and let rest 10 to 15 minutes before cutting.

**Serves 6–8 for lunch or supper**

# Mediterranean Salad

*This salad utilizes gorgeous colored peppers. Fresh sweet basil leaves add a strong flavor reminiscent of peppery licorice—wet, sweet and spicy at the same time. The cilantro and lemon give it a refreshing vitality. Served right after tossing or even after marinating for a day or two, this dish lends itself well to picnics or do-ahead meals. A distinctive flavor of cilantro is pervasive with each bite. Teaming it with a simple cheese quesadilla creates a heavenly combination.*

- **1 tablespoon minced garlic**
- **1 teaspoon cracked pepper**
- **1 tablespoon granulated sugar**
- **1 teaspoon salt**
- **⅛ cup freshly squeezed lemon juice**
- **½ cup olive oil**
- **1 15-ounce can black beans, drained**
- **1 15-ounce can garbanzo beans (chickpeas), drained**
- **1 8-ounce can black olives, drained and sliced**
- **½ cup each: sweet yellow, red, orange, and purple peppers, seeded, and chopped**
- **1 cup fresh blanched or frozen yellow corn kernels**
- **½ cup chopped scallions**
- **½ cup chopped fresh cilantro, leaves only**
- **⅛ cup chopped fresh oregano leaves, or 1 tablespoon dried**

1. Mix together garlic, pepper, sugar, salt, lemon juice, and oil.
2. Place remaining ingredients in a large glass bowl and toss with seasoned oil. Serve immediately or cover and refrigerate for up to 3 days.

**Serves 6–8**

# Marinated Artichokes With Mushrooms

*If you love artichokes and mushrooms, here's one recipe you'll hold on to. Great as an appetizer or as a superb salad when served over mixed greens, this recipe is easily doubled and served differently for two separate occasions. For a super vegetarian supper, it can also be brought to room temperature and tossed with hot fresh pasta.*

- ¼ cup olive oil
- 2 tablespoons fresh lemon juice
- 1 teaspoon granulated sugar
- 1 teaspoon salt
- 1 teaspoon cracked pepper
- 1 teaspoon minced fresh garlic
- 2 tablespoons chopped shallots
- 2 cups artichoke hearts, frozen thawed, or canned drained
- 1 cup hearts of palm, drained and sliced into bite-sized pieces, all tough or fibrous pieces discarded
- 1 cup sliced white mushrooms
- ⅛ cup shredded Romano cheese

1. Mix together oil, lemon juice, sugar, salt, pepper, and garlic.
2. Place remaining ingredients in large glass bowl. Toss with dressing and serve, or cover and refrigerate for up to 3 days.

**Serves 6–8**

# Zucchini And Porcini

This grilled classic is lovely served hot with meats, fish, fowl, and pasta or at room temperature as a first course. Sliced into smaller pieces and served warm over greens, it is a unique luncheon salad. While other mushroom selections may work, the porcini should take a bow. The premium quality porcini mushroom is the Morecci with very dark tops and strong, healthy, light stalks. Its particular smoky flavor comes from its woodsy area of growth.

- **5 6-inch long zucchini, trimmed and sliced in half lengthwise**
- **1½ pounds porcini mushrooms, trimmed of hard stems or brown edges**[*]
- **2 tablespoons olive oil**
- **1 teaspoon salt, or to taste**
- **1 tablespoon cracked pepper**

1. Place all ingredients in a zipper-lock plastic bag. Enclose a good amount of air when sealing and turn gently to coat zucchini and porcini.
2. Cook for 60 seconds on each side over hot coals or under hot broiler.

**Serves 6–8**

---

[*] Grill in large pieces and cut before serving.

*Elegant, Easy and Light*

# Garlic Parmesan Vinaigrette

This is the "house" dressing at our home. The mixture is like a brew, keeping well for up to five days. It not only makes a flavorful salad dressing, but a marvelous marinade for cooked shrimp. Chill and serve poolside for the ultimate in decadence, or toss over sliced cooked steak and stuffed into pitas with shredded lettuce for a delicious sandwich. I have even drizzled it over the top of goat cheese pizzas before and after baking! For sure, it's ahhh-inspiring.

    **1 tablespoon minced garlic**
    **½ cup minced white onion**
    **½ cup grated Parmesan cheese**
    **⅛ cup chopped fresh parsley**
    **1 teaspoon salt, or to taste**
    **1 tablespoon sugar**
    **1 teaspoon cracked pepper, or to taste**
    **¼ cup red wine vinegar**
    **½ cup olive oil**

1. Mix together and toss over mixed greens or cover and refrigerate for up to 5 days.

**Serves 6–8 as a salad dressing**

# Bacon Gorgonzola Vinaigrette

Looking for a rich blend of intense flavors? This succulent dressing does great things to radicchio, Belgian endive, and Romaine lettuce. It's a perfect insalata for any Italian meal, or with the addition of smoked fowl, it is a delectable entree salad. Gorgonzola is a village cheese of beige exterior with a center of blue and grean streaks. Like bleu cheese, it is highly flavorful, especially when aged. Balsamic vinegar is made from the white Trebbiano grape, and its flavor and dark color come from storage in barrels over time.

- ⅓ cup crumbled cooked crisp lean bacon
- 8 ounces Gorgonzola cheese
- ⅛ cup chopped fresh parsley
- 2 tablespoons sugar
- ¼ cup balsamic vinegar
- ½ cup olive oil
- 2 tablespoons cracked pepper

1. Mix together all ingredients and toss with salad selections, or cover and refrigerate for up to 24 hours.

**Serves 6–8**

# Garlic Garbanzo Vinaigrette

*This garlicky dressing, thickened with mashed garbanzos, is unusual but compliment-catching. It makes a super sauce for fried shrimp or clams and a great dip for crudités. Garbanzo beans are also known as ceci beans or chickpeas and have a nutty taste. I find the organic garbanzos, canned with seaweed, to be of extremely high quality and flavor.*

- **½ cup canned garbanzo beans, drained and mashed with the back of a fork**
- **1 tablespoon minced garlic**
- **1 tablespoon paprika**
- **1 tablespoon sugar**
- **1 teaspoon salt, or to taste**
- **1 teaspoon cracked pepper, or to taste**
- **¼ cup red wine vinegar**
- **½ cup olive oil**

1. Mix together all ingredients and serve, or cover and refrigerate for up to 24 hours.

**Serves 6–8 as a salad dressing**

# Honey Lemon Dressing

*Try this sweet but tart dressing over fruit salad or mixed greens. It is also great for dipping chicken bits or doused over a chicken breast sandwich. It is light, yet tangy and refreshing.*

**2 tablespoons mayonnaise**
**½ cup safflower oil**
**⅛ cup red wine vinegar**
**2 tablespoons honey**
**2 tablespoons fresh lemon juice**
**2 tablespoons poppy seeds**
**1 teaspoon Dijon mustard**
**1 tablespoon ketchup**

1. Mix together all ingredients and serve, or cover and refrigerate for up to 24 hours.

**Serves 6–8 as a salad dressing**

# Eggless Caesar Dressing

At our restaurant, Back Bay Gourmet in Tulsa, Oklahoma we made a gallon or more of this for lunch each day! It is tangy but not too tart, with a hint of anchovy, yet without an overpowering fish taste. Increase the anchovies, depending on your own preference.

8 anchovy fillets, patted dry with paper towel
1 tablespoon minced garlic
¼ cup fresh parsley
1 teaspoon Worcestershire sauce
2 tablespoons fresh lemon juice
2 tablespoons cracked pepper
½ cup grated Parmesan cheese
1 teaspoon granulated sugar
⅔ cup olive oil

1. Place all ingredients except olive oil in food processor and pulse until contents are uniformly ground. Scrape down sides.
2. Turn food processor on and slowly pour in olive oil in a thin stream until all oil is used. Process until mixture is thick and homogeneous.
3. Makes enough for 6 to 8 generous salad portions. Romaine is the classic lettuce choice but we love it on all lettuces and most vegetables.

**Yields: Approximately 1½ cups**

# *Italian Salad*

Perfect as a meal all by itself or the perfect prelude to a pasta or hearty soup, this salad is a crowd pleaser. Toss it together without the lettuce and take it to a tailgate with a zipper bagful of prepared Romaine for a final tossing at the last minute. Be sure to keep all ingredients cold in a cooler until serving.

## Dressing

- 1 tablespoon minced garlic
- 2 tablespoons cracked pepper
- 1 tablespoon granulated sugar
- ½ teaspoon crushed Italian-style dried red pepper*
- ½ cup chopped fresh basil
- ⅛ cup chopped fresh oregano, or 1 tablespoon dried
- ¼ cup chopped fresh parsley
- ½ cup chopped red onion
- ¼ cup red wine vinegar
- ¾ cup olive oil

## Salad

- ½ cup oil-cured black olives, pitted and halved
- 1 cup cubed Provolone cheese
- ½ cup grated Parmesan cheese
- ½ cup chopped prepared roasted red peppers, drained
- ½ cup chopped fresh tomato
- ¼ cup chopped pepperoncini
- ½ cup hard Kosher salami, sliced thinly and sliced again into 1-inch strips
- 6 cups coarsely chopped Romaine lettuce

*Continued*

---

\* May be omitted or increased to taste.

1. Mix together dressing ingredients thoroughly and toss with salad ingredients, or cover dressing.
2. Refrigerate for up to 2 days, tossing with salad just before serving.

**Yields: 6–8 generous salads**

**NOTES**

# Tabbouleh Pepper Salad

*Of Middle East origin, Tabbouleh consists primarily of bulghur wheat which is nutty in flavor. This salad is flavored with garlic, lemon, and cilantro, with a hint of mint for a wonderfully full, yet light, flavor. Smoked chicken or beef can be diced and added to this for a marvelous pita stuffer. Leftover Thanksgiving turkey works great. Tabbouleh fans will beg for more.*

## Dressing

1 tablespoon minced garlic
1 teaspoon salt
1 tablespoon granulated sugar
1 tablespoon cracked pepper
1 teaspoon chopped dried mint or 1 tablespoon chopped fresh mint
1 tablespoon dried oregano
¼ cup chopped fresh parsley
¼ cup chopped fresh cilantro
¼ cup red wine vinegar
⅔ cup olive oil

## Salad

1 tablespoon olive oil
½ cup minced white onion
1 tablespoon salt
1 cup bulgar wheat
2 cups water
½ cup chopped red bell pepper
½ cup chopped green bell pepper
½ cup chopped scallions
1 cup crumbled or chopped feta cheese
2 cups finely shredded Romaine lettuce

*Continued*

1. Mix together dressing ingredients thoroughly. Cover and refrigerate.
2. Prepare bulgar wheat by heating oil in heavy saucepan (with a tight-fitting lid) uncovered until hot. Add onion and salt and cook over medium heat until onion begins to brown. Stir in bulgar wheat and cook, stirring constantly, for 30 seconds. Stir in water and continue to stir until water begins to boil. Reduce heat to barely simmering and cover tightly until water is absorbed and wheat is tender but still firm, about 30 to 40 minutes. Remove from heat, stir and cool.
3. Toss dressing with cooled wheat and all remaining ingredients except Romaine. Cover and refrigerate until ready to serve.
4. Serve over a bed of shredded Romaine.

**Serves 6–8**

# Cauliflower Salad

Cauliflower is often overlooked in spite of its availability all year long. This salad is terrific with a club sandwich or served alongside any grilled meat or fish. Growing up in Iowa, I am partial to Maytag Bleu cheese. A chunk of Maytag and some peppered wafer crackers is a true crowd pleaser.

## Dressing

¾ cup mayonnaise
½ cup crumbled bleu cheese
1 tablespoon dried dill
1 tablespoon dried oregano
2 tablespoons red wine vinegar
¼ cup chopped fresh basil
2 tablespoons poppy seeds
2 tablespoons cracked pepper
1 tablespoon sugar

## Salad

3 cups fresh cauliflower flowerettes, rinsed and patted dry
½ cup sun-dried tomatoes prepared in oil, drained and chopped
⅓ cup chopped red onion
½ cup chopped green bell pepper
½ cup pitted black olives, drained and sliced in half

1. Mix together dressing ingredients and pour over salad ingredients. Toss to coat well.
2. Cover and refrigerate until serving. Keeps well for up to 2 days.

**Serves 6–8**

# Tuna Pignolia Salad

My mother makes a fabulous tuna salad that she tops with sliced almonds, which inspired this recipe. It has been savored by ladies at many a luncheon. When we opened our restaurant, Back Bay Gourmet in Tulsa, this was one of our most popular dishes.

> **2 cups fancy albacore tuna packed in spring water, drained**
> **⅔ cup mayonnaise**
> **⅓ cup sweet pickle relish**
> **4 large eggs, hard boiled, peeled and finely chopped or grated**
> **1 tablespoon prepared mustard**
> **½ cup pignolia nuts**[*]
> **Bed of lettuce, or bread for 6 sandwiches**

1. Mix together all ingredients except nuts with a fork, making sure to break up the chunks of tuna. Combine well. Stir in nuts and serve, or cover and refrigerate until ready to serve.

**Serves 6**

---

[*] Available at most supermarkets.

# Indian Tuna Salad

*A spiced-up version of a classic, here's a great pita stuffer. It is neither tame nor mouth-scorching, and is a mainstay for a picnic on the boat on a warm day.*

> 3 cups fancy albacore tuna packed in spring water, drained
> 1 cup mayonnaise
> 4 eggs, hard-boiled, peeled, and finely chopped
> ⅓ cup sweet pickle relish
> 1 teaspoon paprika
> 1 tablespoon mild curry powder
> 1 teaspoon medium-hot curry powder*
> ¼ teaspoon cayenne pepper*
> ½ cup toasted, sliced almonds
> Bed of lettuce, or bread for 6 sandwiches

1. Mix together all ingredients with a fork, making sure to break apart the chunks of tuna. Combine well. Serve, or cover and refrigerate for up to 3 days.

**Serves 6**

---

*May be omitted for the less daring.

# Gingered Carrots

*Gingered carrots, refreshing and different, goes well next to most sandwiches or grilled meats. The combination of ginger and lime brings out the sweetness of the carrots for a wonderful taste. This dish is appealing at a tailgate or by the pool.*

## Dressing

- **2 tablespoons "lite" soy sauce**
- **1 tablespoon freshly grated ginger, or 1 teaspoon powdered**
- **1 teaspoon fresh lime juice**
- **1 teaspoon sesame oil**
- **2 tablespoons granulated sugar**

**4 cups shredded carrots**

1. Mix together dressing ingredients and toss with shredded carrots. Serve immediately or cover and refrigerate for up to 24 hours.

***Serves 4***

# Endive And Lupini Bean Salad

This salad goes well with almost any meal. It's great as is or toss in some chilled cooked shrimp. Lupinis are very salty and must be rinsed in cold water for a good three or four minutes. Then they should be soaked in cold water for ten to fifteen minutes. Lupinis are a yellow, flat Italian bean that add crunch and a delicious wild-like flavor to salads and side dishes and lend themselves well to marinated salads. This salad can be prepared up to two days ahead of time by omitting the endive until just before serving.

## Dressing

- 1 tablespoon minced garlic
- 1 tablespoon granulated sugar
- 2 tablespoons cracked pepper
- ¼ cup red wine vinegar
- ½ cup olive oil
- ½ cup grated Parmesan cheese
- ¼ cup minced white onion

## Salad

- 1½ cups lupini* beans from a jar, rinsed thoroughly and drained
- ½ cup celery, trimmed and sliced into small pieces
- ½ cup prepared roasted red peppers, drained and chopped
- 2 cups Belgian endive, trimmed and sliced into small pieces

1. Mix together all dressing ingredients and toss with salad ingredients. Serve immediately.

**Serves 6–8**

---

* Available at most Italian markets and gourmet specialty stores.

# Vegetable Sandwiches

Don't limit this tasty combination to appetizers. Use larger slices of the bread of your choice for a light and refreshing lunch by the pool or at any picnic. Smoked meat or fowl may be added for extra substance, but this sandwich really stands alone.

- **8 ounces cream cheese, softened**
- **¼ cup minced black olives, drained**
- **¼ cup minced fresh parsley**
- **36 slices cocktail bread**
- **2 ripe avocados, peeled and sliced into small pieces**
- **½ cup mayonnaise**
- **1 tablespoon Dijon mustard**
- **1 cup alfalfa sprouts, rinsed and drained on paper towel**

1. Mix together the cream cheese, olives and parsley. Spread mixture thinly on one side of each piece of bread.
2. Mix together the avocado, mayonnaise, and mustard and divide mixture among 18 of the bread slices.
3. Divide sprouts into 18 clumps and top avocado with sprouts. Place a slice of the remaining bread face down on top of the sprouts to form sandwiches.
4. Cover and refrigerate until ready to serve but no more than 8 hours.

**Serves 8–10 for appetizers**

# Cucumber Tea Sandwiches

These are so elegant, 'veddy' British and quite tasty. They are lovely for a luncheon, as well as arranged on a silver tray garnished with edible flowers. We served them at a Nutcracker Ballet children's tea party for a Tulsa, Oklahoma ballet fund raiser. Everyone applauded.

**24 slices thinly sliced sandwich bread**
**½ cup unsalted butter, softened**
**48 thin slices peeled cucumber**
**1 tablespoon salt, or to taste**
**1 tablespoon paprika**
**2 cups watercress leaves, rinsed and patted dry**

1. Butter one side of each slice of bread. Top 12 of the buttered slices with 4 slices of cucumber each to cover the butter. Sprinkle cucumber with salt and paprika and divide watercress over the top.

2. Place remaining slices of bread, buttered side down to form 12 sandwiches. Trim crust from sandwiches with a sharp knife and cut sandwiches in half diagonally to form triangles.

**Yields: 24 tea sandwiches**

# Cheddar Pea Salad

*A grocery chain where I grew up in Iowa, called Hy Vee, used to make an incredible pea salad. This version comes close, actually is even better. Crab or cocktail shrimp may be added for a luncheon salad.*

> 1 cup mayonnaise, regular or "lite"
> ¼ cup minced sweet gherkins
> 1 tablespoon prepared yellow mustard
> 1 tablespoon celery seed
> 1 tablespoon sweet paprika
> 1 pound frozen young peas
> 1½ cups shredded or chunked mild cheddar cheese

1. Mix together the mayonnaise, gherkins, mustard, celery seed, and paprika.
2. Gently stir in peas while still frozen and the cheese. Cover and refrigerate until ready to serve and peas are thawed. Keeps up to 48 hours.

**Serves 6–8 for lunch or up to 24 for appetizers**

# Caramelized Potatoes

*Sinfully rich, this is a luscious potato dish to serve with roasted or grilled meats, fowl or fish. It is easily made and reheats beautifully.*

> 2 cups potatoes, peeled, quartered, and sliced
> 1 tablespoon salt
> ½ cup unsalted butter
> ¼ cup chopped scallions with greens
> 1 tablespoon cracked pepper
> 1 cup heavy cream or *crème fraiche*\*

1. Place potatoes in deep, heavy saucepan, cover with water, sprinkle salt over top, and bring to simmer over medium heat. Simmer uncovered for 30 minutes. Drain.
2. Heat butter in heavy, nonstick 12- to 14-inch sauté pan over medium-high heat until foam subsides. Add scallions and pepper and sauté for 2 minutes. Stir in potatoes, stir to coat, and press with spatula or back of large spoon into an even layer.
3. Pour cream or *crème fraîche* in an even layer over top of potatoes, spreading with a spoon if needed.
4. Reduce heat to lowest setting and allow to cook, covered loosely with foil, for 1 hour.

**Serves 6–8**

---

\* See Glossary.

*Elegant, Easy and Light*

# Cheesy Spinach

*Even children will eat spinach if you make it with this recipe. Bake it until almost finished and allow to stand, covered, for several hours. Then place it in a 400-degree F. oven for ten minutes just before dinner.*

> ½ cup unsalted butter
> ½ teaspoon minced garlic
> 1 teaspoon salt
> 2 cups frozen chopped spinach, wrung out in a towel and chopped again
> 4 eggs, slightly beaten
> ½ cup cream
> 1 cup shredded fontina cheese
> ¾ cup plain breadcrumbs
> ¾ cup grated Parmesan cheese

1. Heat butter in heavy sauté pan over medium-high heat until foam subsides. Add garlic and salt to pan and stir for 2 minutes. Add spinach and stir 1 minute. Remove from heat and allow to cool.
2. Mix together eggs, cream, and fontina. Stir in spinach and breadcrumbs.
3. Place mixture in an 8" x 12" buttered ovenproof casserole and sprinkle Parmesan over the top.
4. Bake in preheated 350-degree F. oven for 35 to 40 minutes or until puffy and golden.

**Serves 6–8**

# Chicken Salad Louisiana

*Here's a flavorful and appealing salad. Serve in a flaky croissant with a pretty grape cluster for a light lunch, or mound on a platter surrounded by shredded radicchio to make an attractive buffet offering.*

> 1 cup mayonnaise
> ½ cup finely grated hard boiled egg
> ½ cup minced sweet gherkins
> ½ cup chopped celery
> ½ cup chopped scallions with greens
> 1 tablespoon Dijon mustard
> 1 tablespoon cracked pepper
> 1 cup shelled and coarsely chopped pecans
> 3 cups cubed poached, boiled, or grilled white chicken meat

1. Mix together mayonnaise, egg, gherkins, celery, scallions, mustard, and pepper.
2. Stir in pecans and chicken. Cover and refrigerate until ready to serve.

**Serves 6-8**

# Twice Baked Potatoes

*My mother made a version of these for special occasions and often served them with standing rib roast. I learned the art of negotiation during those dinners as we haggled for the largest potato and an end cut from the roast.*

**8 large baking potatoes**
**½ cup unsalted butter**
**¾ cup sour cream**
**½ cup shredded mild cheddar cheese**
**3 eggs, slightly beaten**
**½ cup bacon, fried crisp and crumbled**
**½ cup minced scallions with greens**
**2 teaspoons salt**
**1 tablespoon cracked pepper**

1. Pierce each potato a couple of times with a fork and place directly on rack in middle of preheated 350-degree F. oven for 90 minutes, or until potatoes are tender throughout and skins are crisp.
2. Place the butter in a large glass bowl. Working carefully and wearing a mitt to handle the hot potatoes, cut the top one-fourth off the top of each potato. Carefully scoop out potato from both the top and bottom pieces into the bowl with the butter. When finished scooping all the potatoes, the butter should be melted.
3. Using an electric beater on low setting, mix together the potato flesh, melting butter, sour cream, and cheddar cheese until smooth. Beat in eggs until fluffy.
4. Mix in bacon, scallions, salt, and pepper.
5. Fill each potato shell with whipped mixture and top with potato "lid."
6. Bake on cookie sheet in preheated 350-degree F. oven for 50 minutes or until tops puff up and exposed potato is golden.

**Yields: 8 potatoes**

# Swiss Cheese Potatoes

Loving potatoes as I do, I have tried endless combinations of potatoes with cheese. This version is easy and delicious, and will remind you a little of puffy hashbrowns with cheese. How could that be anything but good?

> 4 eggs, slightly beaten, room temperature
> ½ cup unsalted butter, melted
> ½ cup milk, room temperature
> 1½ cups shredded Swiss cheese
> ½ cup breadcrumbs
> 1 tablespoon cracked pepper
> 1 teaspoon salt
> 4 cups potato, peeled, grated, rinsed in cool water, and drained
> ¾ cup grated Parmesan cheese

1. Mix together the eggs, butter, milk, Swiss cheese, breadcrumbs, cracked pepper, and salt.
2. Combine potatoes with egg mixture and place in a generously buttered 8" x 12" baking dish.
3. Sprinkle Parmesan over top and bake in preheated 350-degree F. oven for 60 minutes or until puffy and golden brown.

**Serves 6–8**

# Chocolate Caramel Fondue

*This is very quick and easy. It makes a handsome presentation with fresh fruit arranged around it. We have made this for New Year's Eve and accompanied it with nothing more than Champagne.*

**12 ounces semisweet chocolate,**
**12 ounces caramels for melting, unwrapped**
**2 tablespoons creme de cacao**\*
**½ cup evaporated milk**
**1 tablespoon water**

1. Place all ingredients in heavy saucepan over medium heat until hot, melted, and smooth. Serve immediately in fondue pot or other container which can be kept warm over a small candle.

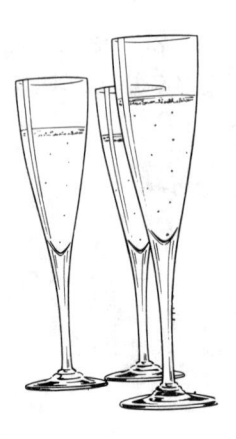

**Yields: About 2 cups**

---

\* A chocolate flavored liqueur which contains vanilla. It is available at most liquor stores.

# Phyllo Pastry With Feta And Spinach

*People request these often, and for good reason — they are positively scrumptious! The tangy, smooth flavor of feta cheese, combined with the spinach between the delicate layers of thin, buttery pastry, is enhanced by garlic and oregano. Assemble ahead of time, cover and freeze right on the baking sheet. If taking directly from the freezer to the oven, reduce oven temperature to 325 degrees F.*

- 1 tablespoon olive oil
- ½ cup minced onion
- ½ tablespoon regular garlic
- 1 tablespoon oregano
- 1 teaspoon salt
- 1 tablespoon cracked pepper
- 1 pound frozen chopped spinach, thawed and wrung out in towel, then chopped again
- ½ cup chopped roasted red peppers
- 1 cup crumbled feta cheese
- ½ cup breadcrumbs
- 36 sheets phyllo pastry
- ½ cup unsalted butter, melted

1. Heat oil in heavy sauté pan over medium-high heat. Stir in onion, garlic, oregano, salt, and pepper and sauté until onion is golden. Stir in spinach and sauté 30 seconds. Remove from heat and let stand for 20 minutes.
2. Stir in roasted peppers, feta, and breadcrumbs. Combine well.
3. Keeping phyllo sheets tightly wrapped until each is used, lay one sheet flat and paint with melted butter with a pastry brush. Fold sheet lengthwise into thirds and paint again with butter.

*Continued*

4. Place a mound of filling about 2 inches from the end of the phyllo strip. Bring corner up so that side is flat with top forming a triangular flap over the filling. Fold down forming another triangle and keep folding to form triangles until strip is used and the filling is enclosed in a triangle of phyllo dough. Paint with butter and place on low-sided baking sheet. Repeat making approximately 36 stuffed triangles.
5. Bake in preheated 350-degree F. oven until puffy, crisp and golden.

**Yields: 36 appetizer portions**

# Basic Quiche With Variations

*When prepared properly, a quiche is a good choice for a luncheon or late supper. ADD: two cups chunked feta cheese and one cup chopped roasted peppers to make a superb Greek-style quiche; one cup smoked chicken, one cup of shredded fontina cheese, and one cup chopped scallions to make an excellent light supper; two cups shredded mild cheddar cheese and one cup small peeled and cleaned shrimp to make an appetizing lunch or first course. If you add a cup of smoked sliced goose to the basic quiche, you will have a unique Christmas Eve supper. The possibilities are limited only by your imagination!*

> 1 pâté brisée*
> 8 eggs
> 1 cup heavy cream
> 1 teaspoon salt
> 1 tablespoon cracked pepper
> ½ teaspoon nutmeg
> 1 cup chopped smoked ham or crumbled crisp bacon
> 2 cups grated Gruyère or fontina cheese
> 3 tablespoons Parmesan cheese
> 2 tablespoons unsalted butter, melted

1. Roll out pastry to about ¼-inch thickness on floured work surface. Roll up over rolling pin and unroll over quiche dish. Trim sides and crimp rim by pinching.
2. Mix together eggs, cream, salt, pepper, and nutmeg with a whisk. Pour one-third of mixture into quiche pan lined with pastry.

*Continued*

---

\* See Glossary

3. Sprinkle the meat in an even layer over the egg mixture. Pour another one-third of the egg mixture over meat. Sprinkle Gruyère in an even layer and pour remaining egg mixture over all.
4. Sprinkle Parmesan over top and drizzle butter over Parmesan.
5. Bake in preheated 350-degree F. oven for 65 minutes or until entire quiche domes up and browns nicely. Quiche will fall when removed from oven.

**Serves 6–8**

# Blackened Chicken Breasts

*This is a simple method to prepare a lean chicken breast that is delicious not only by itself, but also sliced in a tortilla or mixed in a salad. Using skinless breasts and no breading or oils makes it an excellent choice for the calorie-conscious who don't want to sacrifice taste.*

> ¼ cup paprika
> ¼ cup ground cumin
> ¼ cup mild chili powder
> 8 skinless and boneless chicken breast halves
> 1 lemon, halved

1. Mix together paprika, cumin, and chili powder. Dredge chicken pieces to coat well.
2. Heat heavy skillet (seasoned cast iron works great) until very hot. With a pair of tongs, carefully arrange coated chicken pieces in skillet. Cook until chicken begins to blacken on the bottom, about 4 minutes.
3. Turn chicken and cook until juices run clear—about 5 more minutes. Squeeze lemon juice over chicken while still hot in skillet and serve.

**Serves 6–8**

# Veal With Artichokes And Capers

*This is elegant enough for a dinner party entree. It can be assembled ahead of time and baked just before serving. Pounded boneless and skinless chicken breast halves may be substituted for the veal. The salty, tart flavor of the capers and the garlicky, vinegar-enhanced flavor of the marinated artichokes create a memorable combination of flavors.*

**3 eggs**
**2 tablespoons dry sherry**
**8 veal scallopine, pounded to consistent thickness**
**1½ cups breadcrumbs**
**¼ cup olive oil**
**1 teaspoon minced garlic**
**¼ cup unsalted butter**
**½ cup minced onion**
**1 pound mushrooms, sliced**
**1 tablespoon cracked pepper**
**1 tablespoon all-purpose flour**
**1½ cups milk**
**1 cup minced marinated artichoke hearts**
**¼ cup capers, drained**
**1 cup shredded mozzarella cheese**
**½ cup grated Parmesan cheese**

1. Slightly beat the eggs with the sherry and place in bowl with veal. Allow to stand for 30 minutes.
2. Dredge veal pieces in breadcrumbs to coat thoroughly.
3. Heat olive oil in heavy skillet over medium heat with garlic. When garlic begins to turn golden, brown the veal on both sides and arrange on baking tray with sides.
4. With pan still over medium heat, add butter and onion and stir for 1 minute. Reduce heat to medium and stir in mushrooms and pepper. Sauté for 3 minutes.

*Continued*

5. Sprinkle flour over pan and stir for 2 minutes. Continue stirring while slowly pouring in milk. Stir until thick, then stir in artichokes and capers. Pour over veal.
6. Sprinkle mozzarella over veal and sprinkle Parmesan over that. Bake in preheated 350-degree F. oven for about 25 minutes, until cheese is bubbling and brown.

**Serves 6–8**

# Red Veal With Scallops

*The breadcrumbs around the veal absorb the red sauce during the baking, hence the name of this dish. Topping the veal with the sweet bay scallops and smothering it in bubbling cheese is a winning combination. This tantalizing entree can be assembled ahead of time, saving the final baking for just before serving. Served with a salad and good bottle of wine, supper is ready.*

**3 eggs, lightly beaten**
**3 tablespoons sherry**
**8 veal scallopine, pounded thin**
**2 cups breadcrumbs**
**¼ cup olive oil**
**1 teaspoon minced garlic**
**½ cup unsalted butter**
**1 cup minced onion**
**1 pound mushrooms, sliced**
**½ cup chopped basil chopped**
**1 cup tomato paste**
**2 tablespoons granulated sugar**
**1 teaspoon salt**
**1 tablespoon cracked pepper**
**1 cup sweet red wine**
**1 pound bay scallops, rinsed and patted dry**
**1 cup shredded mozzarella cheese**
**½ cup grated Parmesan cheese**

1. Mix together eggs and sherry and allow veal to soak in the mixture for 30 minutes. Dredge veal in breadcrumbs to coat.
2. Heat oil with garlic in large, heavy sauté pan over medium-high heat and brown both sides of veal. Arrange on baking sheet with sides.

*Continued*

3. In same unwashed sauté pan over medium-high heat, place butter and onion. Sauté for 4 minutes and stir in mushrooms. Sauté 1 minute more. Stir in basil, tomato paste, sugar, salt, and pepper and reduce heat to medium-low. Stir in wine. Simmer for 2 minutes and pour over veal.
4. Divide scallops into small mounds on each piece of veal. Sprinkle mozzarella over the veal and Parmesan over that.
5. Place in preheated 350-degree F. oven for 30 minutes or until cheese is brown and bubbly.

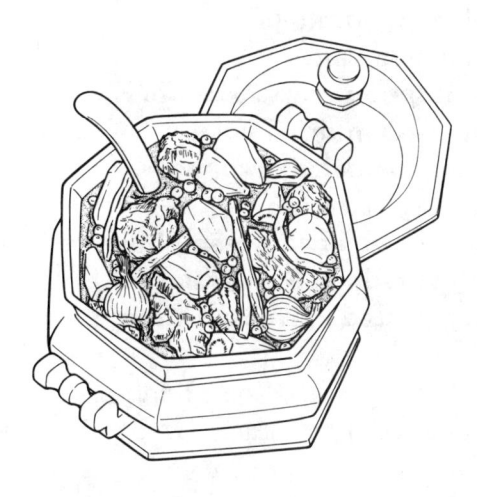

**Serves 6–8**

# Poulet Suisse

This is one of my sister Andrea's favorite dishes, and I make it for her whenever we are together. I created it when we were living on a small farm outside of Des Moines. My sister was coming for supper but Laurie and I did not want to go to the market, so we concocted this from what we had in the house. We always keep some chicken breasts in the freezer for just such an emergency.

- 3 eggs, lightly beaten
- 3 tablespoons dry sherry
- 8 chicken breast halves, skinned and boned
- 2 cups breadcrumbs
- ¼ cup olive oil
- 1 teaspoon minced garlic
- ½ cup unsalted butter
- 1 cup minced onion
- 1 cup tomato paste
- 2 tablespoons sugar
- 1 teaspoon salt
- 1 tablespoon cracked pepper
- 1 tablespoon dried basil
- 1 teaspoon dried oregano
- 1 cup dry red wine
- 1 cup sliced small green pimiento-stuffed olives
- 1 cup shredded Swiss cheese
- ½ cup grated Parmesan cheese

1. Mix together eggs and sherry and allow chicken to soak in the mixture for 30 minutes. Dredge in breadcrumbs to coat.
2. Heat oil with garlic in large, heavy sauté pan over medium-high heat and brown both sides of chicken. Arrange on baking sheet with sides.

*Continued*

3. In same unwashed sauté pan over medium-high heat, add butter and onion. Sauté for 5 minutes. Stir in tomato paste, sugar, salt, pepper, basil, and oregano and reduce heat to medium-low. Stir in wine. Simmer for 2 minutes and pour over chicken.
4. Divide olives into small mounds on each piece of chicken. Sprinkle Swiss cheese over the chicken and Parmesan over that.
5. Place in preheated 350-degree F. oven for 30 minutes or until cheese is brown and bubbly.

**Serves 6–8**

## Veal With Prosciutto

*It will be hard to find a guest who isn't thrilled when this mouth-watering dish is served. Chicken substituted for the veal works nicely. It can be assembled ahead of time, leaving the baking until just before serving. Prosciutto is a raw ham that has been salt-cured and aged. Full in flavor, it must be sliced paper thin. The most heavenly are from Parma.*

- 3 eggs, lightly beaten
- 3 tablespoons sherry
- 8 veal scallopine, pounded thin
- 2 cups breadcrumbs
- ¼ cup olive oil
- 1 teaspoon minced garlic
- ½ cup unsalted butter
- 1 cup minced onion
- 1 pound mushrooms, sliced
- ½ cup chopped basil
- 1 cup tomato paste
- 2 tablespoons granulated sugar
- 1 teaspoon salt
- 1 tablespoon cracked pepper
- 1 cup dry red wine
- 8 large slices prosciutto ham
- 1 cup shredded fontina cheese
- 1 cup grated Parmesan cheese

1. Mix together eggs and sherry and allow veal to soak in the mixture for 30 minutes. Dredge veal in breadcrumbs to coat.
2. Heat oil with garlic in large, heavy sauté pan over medium-high heat and brown both sides of veal. Set aside.

*Continued*

3. In same unwashed sauté pan over medium-high heat, add butter and onion. Sauté for 4 minutes and stir in mushrooms. Sauté 1 minute more. Stir in basil, tomato paste, sugar, salt, and pepper and reduce heat to medium-low. Stir in wine. Simmer for 2 minutes and pour over bottom of baking dish large enough to accommodate the veal.
4. Arrange veal on top of sauce and place a piece of prosciutto over each piece of veal. Sprinkle fontina over the prosciutto and Parmesan over that.
5. Place in preheated 350-degree F. oven for 30 minutes or until cheese is brown and bubbly.

**Serves 6–8**

*Chapter IV*

# THE COCKTAIL BUFFET

Preparing ahead and planning allows you time for drinking, eating and conversation. It allows you to show off your special entertaining skills by creating and presenting a broad selection of dishes.

Simple things, like a bleu cheese tart and cilantro tortilla roll-ups, can be combined with more complicated dishes such as spring rolls and thrice-cooked ribs to make preparation easier. If you're too busy to prepare everything yourself, then combine your own creations with specialty items created by your favorite gourmet store or local caterer. Try to bake and freeze sweets earlier in the month. Purchase imported chocolates for your dessert table. Arrange them with fresh flowers and rose petals for a dynamite effect.

Hiring a few people to help serve, tend bar and clean up will enable you to enjoy yourself throughout the event and afterwards. But if this is not possible, start your preparations early on so you can enjoy the party as much as your guests!

*Chapter IV*

# THE COCKTAIL BUFFET
## Recipe List

*Stuffed Mushroom Caps*
*Clam Stuffed Mushrooms*
*Roasted Garlic Goat Cheese Tart*
*Goat Cheese Tart with Caramelized Onions*
*Hummus*
*Apricot Bleu Cheese Dip*
*Smoked Salmon Pâté*
*Smoked Oyster Pâté*
*Chicken Drumsticks*
*Hot Ginger Sauce*
*Basil Cheese Toasts*
*Candied Lamb in Phyllo*
*Bleu Cheese Pie*
*Marinated Sweet Peppers*
*Pineapple Crab Mousse*
*Marinated Goat Cheese*
*Bunderfleisch Scallion Rolls*
*Tuna Antipasto*
*Three Cheese Torte*
*Tapenade*
*Brie with Apricots in Puff Pastry*

*Continued*

*Bleu Cheese Balls*
*Asparagus Tips in Pine Nuts*
*Chicken Liver Pâté with Cognac, Apple, and Truffles*
*Red and White Cabbage Relish*
*Caviar Egg Salad*
*Italian White Bean Salad*
*Lupini Bean Salad*
*Caviar Cucumber Salad*
*Pumpernickel Pizzas*
*Creamy Carrot Salad*
*Spinach Pancakes*
*Potato Pancakes*
*Buckwheat Blinis*
*Whole Beef Tenderloin with Raspberry Sauce*
*Toasted Onion Chicken*
*American Foo Young*
*Blueberry Rhubarb Chutney*
*Stuffed Dipped Apricots*
*Cold Stuffed Lobster Tails*
*Clam Stuffed Chicken Breasts*
*Stuffed Sirloin Roll*
*Herbed Scallops with Smoked Salmon*
*Basil Cream Sauce*
*Chicken Liver Omelette*
*Crêpes and Variations*
*Poached Pears and Variations*

# Stuffed Mushroom Caps

*Edible containers are a plus at parties. Not only do they look good, but they are small enough to munch in one or two bites. Assemble several hours ahead and refrigerate to leave time for other last-minute chores. These are particularly flavorful from the use of many fresh herbs and a hint of garlic and red wine. They melt in your mouth and are always a hit.*

**24 large white mushrooms***
**1 tablespoon olive oil**
**1 teaspoon salt**
**½ cup sweet unsalted butter**
**2 tablespoons safflower oil, or other light oil**
**½ cup minced onion**
**1½ teaspoons minced garlic**
**2 tablespoons chopped fresh parsley**
**2 tablespoons chopped fresh basil**
**1 tablespoon chopped fresh oregano, or 1 teaspoon dried**
**1 tablespoon cracked pepper**
**¼ cup tomato paste**
**2 tablespoons granulated sugar**
**¼ cup dry red wine**
**½ cup plain breadcrumbs**

1. Gently break stems away from mushroom caps. Rinse the caps, pat dry, and place in zipper-lock bag with olive oil and salt. Gently shake to coat, then place on an ovenproof serving dish.
2. Trim bottoms from stems, rinse and pat dry. Mince.

*Continued*

---

* About 1½ to 2 inches in diameter.

3. Heat butter and safflower oil in heavy sauté pan until foam subsides. Add minced stems, onion, garlic, parsley, basil, oregano, and pepper. Sauté while gently mixing with spoon for 2 to 3 minutes over medium-high heat. Reduce heat to low and stir in tomato paste, sugar, and wine. Cook and stir for 1 minute more and add breadcrumbs to mixture. Remove from heat.
4. Divide filling among caps and bake in preheated 350-degree F. oven for 25 minutes or until tops are browned. Serve hot or at room temperature.

**Serves 6–8 as a first course**

# Clam Stuffed Mushrooms

*These stuffed mushrooms are superb and taste similar to escargot — heavy garlic with the delicate flavor of butter and the marvelous texture of clams. We have never had any left over.*

- **24 2-inch diameter white mushrooms**
- 1 tablespoon olive oil
- 1 teaspoon salt
- 1 tablespoon cracked pepper
- 1 cup unsalted butter
- ¼ cup minced shallots
- 1 tablespoon minced garlic
- 2 tablespoons chopped fresh parsley
- ¾ cups minced fresh shucked clams
- ¼ cup white wine
- ½ cup plain breadcrumbs
- ½ cup grated Parmesan cheese

1. Separate mushroom caps from stems by gently breaking off the stems. Rinse the caps, pat dry and place in zipper-lock bag with olive oil, salt and pepper. Gently shake to coat, then arrange on an ovenproof serving dish.
2. Trim bottoms from stems, rinse, and pat dry. Mince.
3. Heat butter in heavy sauté pan over medium-high heat until foam subsides. Add minced stems, shallots, garlic, and parsley. Sauté while gently mixing with spoon for 2 to 3 minutes over medium-high heat.
4. Reduce heat to medium and stir in clams. Cook and stir for 2 minutes more.
5. Reduce heat to low and add wine, stirring well. Finally add breadcrumbs to mixture. Remove from heat.
6. Divide filling among caps and top each with Parmesan. Bake in preheated 350-degree F. oven for 25 minutes; tops should be brown. Serve hot or at room temperature.

**Serves 6–8 as an appetizer**

# Roasted Garlic Goat Cheese Tart

Combinations of garlic and goat cheese are endless. When the garlic is roasted, it becomes romantic and a sort of comfort food. With crusty French bread, or crisp garlic toasts, it's just about all you need. Well, maybe a bottle of vino.

Goat cheese is white in color and really made from goat's milk. Imported chèvre, usually from France, is more tart and crumbly than domestic. I prefer the domestic, for almost every state in the U.S. has its own local goat cheese maker whose product is consistently smooth and creamy. Goat cheese most often comes in a log shape and is offered plain or covered in pepper, herbs or ashes. My favorite is Texas Goat Cheese (see sources) made by the Mozzarella Company in Dallas. Seal Cove Goat Cheese made in Northeast Maine is also superb.

**1 head elephant garlic**
**½ teaspoon olive oil**
**1 teaspoon salt, or to taste**
**½ cup butter, room temperature**
**2 tablespoons cracked pepper**
**1 teaspoon salt**
**1 pound fresh soft goat cheese**
**½ cup chopped pecans**

1. Place garlic on aluminum foil and drizzle with olive oil and 1 teaspoon salt. Loosely wrap foil around garlic allowing garlic to show freely on top. Place in 350-degree F. oven for 1 hour or until garlic feels soft when pressed. Remove from oven and fold foil tightly around garlic. Allow to stand at room temperature for 20 minutes.

2. Remove paperlike wrapping from garlic cloves and trim off any tough root ends. Place in food processor with butter, pepper, and salt. Pulse until the consistency of chutney.

3. Place goat cheese at the center of a serving plate and press into 1-inch thick, flat, round disk. Frost goat cheese with garlic-butter mixture and press pecans into sides to appear as "crust." Serve at room temperature.

**Serves 6–8 as an appetizer or 12–18 at an appetizer buffet**

# Goat Cheese Tart With Caramelized Onions

*Ambrosia. Heaven on earth. Incredible. Phenomenal. And easy, too. This quick crust is my creation. It is crisp and delicious with a buttery combination of garlic and pepper. It can also be used for quiche. The caramelizing of the onions gives them a deep golden-brown color and rich full flavor.*

## Crust

- 8 large shredded wheat puffs
- ½ cup unsalted butter, cut into tablespoon size pieces and softened
- 1 teaspoon minced garlic
- 1 teaspoon salt
- 1 tablespoon cracked pepper

## Filling

- 1 pound fresh soft goat cheese
- 4 eggs at room temperature
- 3 tablespoons heavy cream

## Caramelized Onion Topping

- ½ cup unsalted butter
- 2 cups sweet onions, cut into 2-inch long strips
- ½ cup minced shallots
- 1 tablespoon salt
- 1 tablespoon cracked pepper
- ⅛ cup sherry
- ½ cup grated Parmesan cheese

1. Break up shredded wheat puffs and place them into a food processor bowl fitted with a steel blade. Add the remaining crust ingredients. Pulse until contents resemble coarse meal.

*Continued*

2. Scraping bowl with a spatula, empty wheat mixture into 11-inch or 12-inch fluted, false bottomed, metal tart pan. Press into sides first and then in an even layer over the bottom. Set aside.

3. Return unwashed bowl and blade to food processor and place filling contents in bowl. Pulse until mixture is smooth, scraping sides of bowl once or twice as needed. Spoon mixture into crust and gently work filling into a smooth layer.

4. To make onion topping, heat butter in large skillet until foam subsides. Add onions, shallots, salt, and pepper to pan and sauté over medium-high heat while stirring until onions are clear and soft. Stir in sherry. Stir for 30 seconds more and remove from heat. Spread over goat cheese filling in an even layer and sprinkle Parmesan cheese over onions.

5. Bake in preheated 350-degree F. oven for 50 to 60 minutes or until filling swells into a dome and cheese is quite brown. Tart filling will fall when removed from oven. Allow to stand 10 minutes before removing side of pan and cutting tart.

**Serves 6–8 as a first course or 16 for a buffet**

# Hummus

Hummus is a blend of chick peas, garlic, and lemon or lime juice that originated in the Middle East and can be spiced up to your own taste. The traditional version is bound with olive oil, but this recipe uses non-fat yogurt for a fresh and light result. It is quite successful as part of a crudité or inside mini-pitas with a few alfalfa sprouts on a silver tray at a cocktail buffet. Attractive and easy presentations like this are a must when entertaining large groups.

> **1 15-ounce can garbanzo beans (chickpeas), drained**
> **½ teaspoon garlic, minced**
> **1 teaspoon ground cumin**
> **1 teaspoon mild chili powder**
> **1 tablespoon lime juice**
> **⅛ cup chopped fresh cilantro**
> **1 teaspoon salt**
> **1 teaspoon cracked pepper**
> **1 teaspoon paprika**
> **⅛ cup olive oil**
> **½ cup plain non-fat yogurt**

1. Place all ingredients except yogurt into food processor fitted with steel blade. Pulse using 3-second pulses until mixture is like the texture of cornmeal, scraping down sides as needed. Add yogurt to bowl and pulse until smooth.

**Yields: 6–8 large sandwiches, or will serve 10–12 as a dip**

# Apricot Bleu Cheese Dip

*Sounds odd? You cannot imagine the combination? Try it once and I guarantee it will be a staple. With chips, vegetables, or spread on toasts topped with caviar, this is fabulous and easy.*

- **1 8-ounce package cream cheese, softened**
- **½ cup crumbled bleu cheese**
- **½ cup apricot preserves**
- **¼ cup chopped scallions**
- **1 tablespoon paprika**
- **1 teaspoon Worcestershire sauce**
- **Caviar for topping (optional)**

1. Place all ingredients into food processor fitted with a steel blade. Pulse until lumpy but beginning to smooth, scraping down sides as needed.

**Yields: About 2 cups**

# Smoked Salmon Pâté

A classic at any brunch, this pâté is delicious with bagels or on bagel chips. Smooth it onto pumpernickel bread, add a slice of tomato, and it becomes an elegant tailgate event. It is a focal point of a cocktail buffet table on a silver tray surrounded by flowers and assorted crackers. Use smoked Scottish salmon or Nova lox from the delicatessen.

> **1 8-ounce package cream cheese, softened**
> **½ pound smoked salmon, sliced**
> **¼ cup chopped white onion**
> **1 tablespoon paprika**

1. Place all ingredients into food processor fitted with a steel blade. Pulse until smooth, scraping down sides as needed.

**Yields: About 2 cups**

# Smoked Oyster Pâté

A version of this was kept in a pastry bag fitted with a fluted tip at all times in the restaurant we owned in Tulsa, Oklahoma, Back Bay Gourmet. This is very simplistic, but elegant, with little toasts or when piped into hollowed cherry tomatoes. It keeps well up to three days in the refrigerator.

- 1 8-ounce package cream cheese, softened
- ½ cup smoked oysters, drained
- ¼ cup chopped white onion
- 1 teaspoon paprika

1. Place all ingredients into food processor fitted with a steel blade. Pulse until smooth, scraping down sides as needed.

**Yields: About 2 cups**

## Chicken Drumsticks

*Anything fried and crispy is usually my first stop at a cocktail buffet. Remember to always change plates, so to leave no evidence of the number consumed. This batter that combines peanut butter and cilantro can cause an argument over who gets the last one.*

> 24 chicken wings
> 2 tablespoons soy sauce
> ¼ cup cornstarch
> 2 tablespoons rice vinegar*
> 2 tablespoons milk
> 2 tablespoons creamy peanut butter
> 4 eggs, slightly beaten
> ¼ cup unbleached all-purpose flour
> 1 tablespoon cracked pepper
> ⅛ cup chopped fresh cilantro
> 1 cup safflower oil, or other light oil, for frying
> Hot Ginger Sauce (page 101)

1. With a very sharp knife, meat cleaver, or poultry shears, separate drumstick portion of wing from other two pieces, reserving the latter for chicken stock or other use. For family you may use the whole wing, but for cocktail parties the drumstick alone works best. Toss drumsticks with soy sauce and set aside.

2. Mix cornstarch with vinegar and milk until smooth. Stir in peanut butter and gradually add eggs. Stir in flour, pepper, and cilantro.

3. Heat oil in deep sauté pan until hot, but not smoking, over medium-high heat. A good test for the readiness of the oil is to drop a small piece of white bread into the hot oil. It should bubble and turn golden in 45 seconds or less.

*Continued*

---

*Available at Oriental markets.

4. Have the drumsticks near the oil and, holding the batter mixture, dip each drumstick in the batter and carefully set into the hot oil. Repeat with up to one-half of the drumsticks. Turn each when golden brown, cooking about 5 minutes per side. Hold in 200-degree F. oven on paper towel-lined pan until remaining drumsticks are battered and fried. Serve warm with *Hot Ginger Sauce* (to follow).

**Yields: 24**
**Serves 6–8 as a first course, 15 at a cocktail buffet**

# Hot Ginger Sauce

Here is a multi-purpose dipping sauce for most Oriental appetizers, or dim sum, those awesome Oriental tidbits of decadence. It is also a winner with grilled meats, fish, and roasted fowl, as the hot, sweet, gingery flavor brings out the taste buds. For a thicker, sweeter sauce, stir in two tablespoons of apricot preserves.

- **3 tablespoons soy sauce**
- **½ teaspoon hot oil***
- **1 teaspoon sesame oil**
- **1 tablespoon garlic bean sauce**
- **1 tablespoon peeled minced ginger root**
- **1 teaspoon granulated sugar**
- **1 tablespoon minced scallions or chives**

1. Combine all ingredients to blend, cover and refrigerate until serving. Bring to room temperature to serve. Keeps up to 10 days in the refrigerator.

**Yields: ½ cup**

---

* Available at most Oriental markets.

# Basil Cheese Toasts

*These are based on a recipe given to my mother by a wonderful woman, Betty Krantz, from Des Moines, Iowa. I use these, or a version thereof, at almost every party. Besides being the perfect solution for cheese spreads, dips, and canapés, they complement soups and salads. They keep well in a tightly-sealed plastic container for up to a week.*

**1 cup unsalted butter, melted**
**1 loaf mini-cocktail-sliced pumpernickel or rye bread**
**1 tablespoon dried basil**
**1 tablespoon dried oregano**
**1 tablespoon dried parsley**
**1 cup shredded Parmesan cheese**

1. Paint generously with butter the bottom of the largest jelly-roll pan or cookie sheet that will fit into your oven. Arrange as many slices of the bread as will lie flat on the pan.
2. Using the pastry brush, cover the top of each bread slice and sprinkle with herbs first, and then cheese.
3. Bake in preheated 375-degree F. oven for about 40 minutes or until toasts are browned and crispy. Place on paper towel, loosely wrap with aluminum foil, and hold in warm oven until ready to serve. It is not necessary to wash the pan between batches of toasts if all of the bread slices will not fit on the tray.

**Yields: About 36 toasts**

# Candied Lamb In Phyllo

*This crowd pleaser will make your guests ask how many days you spent cooking. They need not know it only took a little time by using shortcut-style recipes like this one.*

> 1 tablespoon olive oil
> 1 teaspoon minced garlic
> 1 pound ground lamb
> 1 tablespoon cracked pepper, or to taste
> 1 teaspoon salt, or to taste
> ½ cup granulated sugar
> ½ cup white corn syrup
> 1 tablespoon water
> 2 tablespoons minced fresh ginger
> 2 tablespoons fresh lime juice
> 24 sheets phyllo pastry, room temperature and covered with plastic
> ½ cup melted butter

1. Heat oil and garlic in heavy sauté pan over medium-high heat until garlic begins to brown. Stir in lamb and continue to cook meat until well-browned and dry. Remove from heat and set aside.

2. In small heavy saucepan, heat while gently stirring the sugar, corn syrup and water over medium-high until mixture begins to boil. Reduce heat to medium and cease stirring. Boil about 15 minutes or until between soft and hardball stage on candy thermometer. Remove from heat and stir in ginger and lime juice. Pour mixture over lamb and stir to coat thoroughly.

3. Paint the bottom of a large jelly roll pan or cookie sheet with melted butter using a pastry brush. Remove a sheet of the phyllo pastry from the plastic wrap, resealing as you use each piece, and paint with butter. Fold lengthwise into thirds.

*Continued*

4. Place approximately 1 tablespoon of the lamb about an inch from the end of the folded pastry. Fold a corner of the pastry over the filling, bringing the end of the pastry in line with the top, forming a triangle flap. Fold triangle including filling down to form another triangle and continue to fold until a single triangle of folded dough is formed and the filling is enclosed. Place on pan. Repeat using balance of phyllo and filling, painting the tops of the triangles with butter upon completion of the tray. These may be covered and refrigerated for up to 2 days at this point.
4. Bake in preheated 350-degree F. oven until pastry is golden brown and the butter is bubbling.

**Yields: 24  3" triangle-shaped pastries**

# Bleu Cheese Pie

Imagine the tangy taste of bleu cheese spiced with pepper and scallions baked in a pecan crust. This is an absolutely scrumptious appetizer. It is beautiful to present to your guests and so very easy to make. The sour cream topping brings out a smoothness in the texture of the cheese that contrasts with the crunch in the nutty crust.

1 cup shelled pecan halves
1 cup cornflakes
½ cup unsalted butter, cut into chunks
1 tablespoon cracked pepper
1 teaspoon salt
8 ounces cream cheese, softened
8 ounces bleu cheese, crumbled or chunked
½ cup chopped scallions
3 eggs, slightly beaten
1 cup sour cream

1. In food processor fitted with steel blade pulse the pecans, cornflakes, butter, pepper, and salt until the texture of coarse meal. Press in an even layer into bottom and sides of 11-inch false-bottomed tart pan.

2. Wipe processor bowl and blade with paper towel and return to base. Pulse cream cheese, bleu cheese, scallions, and eggs until smooth, scraping down sides as needed.

3. Pour cheese mixture into crust and bake in preheated 350-degree F. oven for 40 to 50 minutes. Filling should swell up into a dome when cooked and fall upon removal from oven. Immediately after removing, carefully spread sour cream over top and allow to cool to room temperature before cutting and serving.

**Yields: 8 pie-shaped wedges, or 16–20 appetizers**

# Marinated Sweet Peppers

*Right out of an Italian café, these sweet peppers require only the closing of one's eyes for a quick visit to Italia. Fresh-cooked spaghetti tossed with these diced, marinated peppers can be served hot or cold. Use over crostini smothered in goat cheese, along with fresh mozzarella, or as a mainstay on homemade pizza. The marinade is sweetened with a touch of sugar, spiked with garlic, and laced with basil for a palate-pleasing combination.*

**12 assorted sweet peppers, quartered, seeded, and trimmed**
**1 teaspoon minced garlic**
**⅛ cup olive oil**
**1 teaspoon granulated sugar**
**1 teaspoon salt**
**1 tablespoon cracked pepper**
**⅛ cup minced fresh basil**

1. Roast and skin peppers.

2. Mix together oil, sugar, salt, pepper, and basil in a glass or ceramic bowl large enough to accommodate peppers. Toss with peppers, cover and refrigerate. Serve room temperature.

**Serves 6–8 as a first course or side dish or up to 24 for appetizers**

# Pineapple Crab Mousse

*This may sound like an odd combination, but it is fabulous. Serve atop shredded greens for a refreshing summer treat. With assorted crackers, or spread on cocktail bread, it may become habitual.*

- **2 tablespoons powdered gelatin**
- **½ cup boiling water**
- **12 ounces cream cheese**
- **1 cup fresh boiled crabmeat, or canned, picked over for shell and rinsed**
- **1 cup canned crushed pineapple, drained and wrung dry in a kitchen towel**
- **½ cup chopped red onion**
- **1 tablespoon Worcestershire sauce**
- **½ cup chopped walnuts**

1. Dissolve gelatin in boiling water.
2. Place remaining ingredients in food processor fitted with steel blade. Pulse to mix. Turn processor on and add dissolved gelatin in a stream. Scrape down sides and process 10 seconds more.
3. Pour into oiled 1-quart ring mold. Refrigerate until solid, several hours or overnight. Dip bottom and sides of mold, keeping contents dry, into hot water for 20 seconds. Cover top of mold with serving platter and invert. Shake mold and plate together to loosen mousse if necessary.

**Serves 8–10 for lunch or 24 for appetizers**

# Marinated Goat Cheese

Slice logs of goat cheese with white sewing thread or unwaxed fine dental floss. Molding soft goat cheese is easier and allows for more appropriate sizing according to the occasion. One-inch balls are suitable for appetizers while three-inch patties atop shredded greens are excellent for lunch or for a first/salad course. These hold well in the refrigerator for up to five days.

- **1 pound domestic or imported goat cheese, sliced or molded**
- **½ cup olive oil**
- **⅛ cup red wine vinegar**
- **1 teaspoon granulated sugar**
- **1 teaspoon salt**
- **1 tablespoon cracked pepper**
- **⅛ cup minced fresh basil**
- **⅛ cup minced fresh parsley**
- **½ teaspoon minced garlic**

1. Arrange goat cheese in shallow 8½" x 11" glass baking dish or on shallow serving platter.
2. Mix together balance of ingredients and pour over cheese. Cover and refrigerate. Bring to room temperature to serve. Serve on platter or arrange atop of shredded radicchio.

**Serves 6–8 for lunch or up to 24 for appetizers**

# Bundnerfleisch Scallion Rolls

*My mother- and father-in-law brought us some mouth-watering air-dried meat, called Bundnerfleisch, from Switzerland. Sliced paper thin and tightly wrapped, it has a great smoke flavor. Any lean smoked ham will work, but Bundnerfleish can be found at a specialty market.*

**24 scallions, greens removed, leaving approximately 5 inches of onion**
**24 pieces Bundnerfleisch or smoked ham, very thinly sliced**
**24 wooden toothpicks**

1. Tightly roll a scallion in each slice of meat and secure with a toothpick.
2. Heat a heavy nonstick skillet over high heat and grill each bundle on two sides until browned and edges begin to crisp. Serve warm.

**Yields: 24 6" rolls**

# Tuna Antipasto

This is a version of my mother's recipe. She used pearl onions from a jar, which does not thrill me, and I make mine spicier with the chili powder which she ommitted. This is a wonderful blend of vegetables, olives, tuna and horseradish in a red chili sauce. It can be made the day before and keeps for five days in the refrigerator. Loved by almost everyone, this dish is very low in fat, spicy but not overpowering, and is delicious over shredded greens for lunch.

> **16 ounces fancy albacore white meat tuna in spring water**
> 1 cup bottled chili sauce
> 1 teaspoon mild chili powder
> ⅛ cup prepared horseradish
> 1 teaspoon cracked pepper
> 1 tablespoon fresh lemon juice
> 1 cup chunked pickled cauliflower, drained
> 1 cup sliced pitted green olives, drained
> ½ cup chunked seeded sweet red pepper
> ¼ cup chopped onion

1. Mix together tuna, chili sauce, chili powder, horseradish, cracked pepper, and lemon juice with a fork to break up chunks of tuna. Stir in remaining ingredients.
2. Cover and refrigerate until serving.

**Serves 6–8, or up to 24 for appetizers**

# Three Cheese Torte

*This is truly a remarkable torte that is so easy but looks like you just graduated from a cooking class in Europe. It can be made up to five days ahead but must be made at least one day prior to serving. The combination of these smooth cheeses looks so beautiful when the torte is cut, exposing their glory. Serve whole on a decorative platter garnished with Greek olives and roasted peppers, or slice and present atop shredded greens for a "knock 'em over" first or salad course.*

> **2 pounds fresh domestic goat cheese**
> **½ cup pine nuts**
> **1 cup chopped fresh basil**
> **2 pounds provolone cheese, thinly sliced**
> **2 pounds Muenster cheese, thinly sliced**
> **½ cup unsalted butter, melted**

1. Line a 5" x 11" glass loaf-shaped baking dish with plastic wrap.
2. Mix goat cheese with pine nuts and basil.
3. Layer one-third each of the provolone and Muenster cheeses in the bottom of the lined dish. Paint between each layer with butter and press with fingertips. Spoon in one-half of the goat cheese mixture and spread evenly, eliminating any air pockets.
4. Layer another one-third of the provolone and Muenster as before, painting each slice with butter. Spoon the remaining goat cheese mixture over and again spread evenly. Top with the remaining cheese, alternating provolone and Muenster and again painting between each slice. Cover with plastic wrap.

*Continued*

5. If the torte does not stand at least one-half inch above the glass dish, cut a piece of cardboard to the shape of the top of the dish and place on top until reaching a height above the sides of the pan. Weight the top with a large, heavy book and refrigerate overnight or longer.
6. Unmold loaf by lifting plastic wrap liner and inverting onto serving tray.

**Serves 16–24 for appetizerss**

# Tapenade

*Known as poor man's caviar or olive pâté, this is a savory spread for a crisp slice of French bread. It also makes an appetizing garnish for fresh mozzarella and is super with grilled meats. For cocktails, serve on simple crackers or grilled toasts. Oil-cured olives are rich and strong in flavor, adding a Mediterranean flair to this spread. They are found jarred in most gourmet stores or in bulk at larger international delicatessens. Your guests will beg you for the recipe.*

> **2 cups pitted oil-cured black olives**
> **1 2-ounce tin anchovy fillets, drained**
> **½ teaspoon minced garlic**
> **1 teaspoon dried oregano**
> **1 tablespoon extra virgin olive oil**

1. Place all ingredients in food processor fitted with steel blade. Pulse until the texture of mashed potatoes. Cover and refrigerate until ready to serve. Serve at room temperature. You might garnish with shredded Asiago cheese for appetizers.

**Serves 24 as an appetizer**

# Brie With Apricots In Puff Pastry

A surefire way to gather a crowd around the table is to serve this toothsome combination. I learned how to make this from my mentor, Melva Bucksbaum, with whom I taught my first cooking class. This version uses frozen puff pastry because it is so easy and works so well, whereas Melva would make it from scratch. One can also purchase raw puff pastry from a good French bakery for superior results. But rest assured, there was never a complaint when using the frozen! Triple-cream Brie is the richest there is and is a heavenly rich combination with the delicate pastry and sweet apricots. Double-cream Brie will work almost as well.

> 1 8-ounce jar apricot preserves
> 12 ounces dried apricot halves, cut into quarters
> 2 pounds fresh or frozen puff pastry rolled into two equal circles, four inches larger than the Brie
> 1 2- or 3-pound whole triple-cream Brie wheel*
> 1 egg yolk, slightly beaten with 1 teaspoon water

1. Place preserves and apricots into small sauce pan over medium-low heat and bring to a simmer. Reduce heat to low and simmer for 10 minutes. Remove from heat.
2. Place one sheet of pastry over the bottom of a tart pan or false-bottomed cake pan that is an inch larger than the Brie. Place Brie on the pastry and spread the apricot mixture over the top in an even layer.

*Continued*

---

\* Double-cream will work. Use any cow's milk cheese enriched with cream; minimum of 60% butterfat.

3. Fold pastry up around Brie and paint with egg. Lay the other piece of pastry over the top and gently press the edges of both pastry pieces together in order to seal. Make a small "X" in the center with the tip of a sharp knife, cutting almost, but not completely, through to the apricots. Paint completed pastry with egg.
4. Bake on cookie sheet in preheated 350-degree F. oven for 40 minutes or until pastry is puffed and brown. Serve warm.

**Serves 6–8 or up to 24 for appetizers**

# Bleu Cheese Balls

*These can be made ahead of time and are easy to make in a short time. Instead of always rolling in pecans, you might want to diversify with minced parsley, paprika, or chopped scallion greens.*

**16 ounces cream cheese, softened**
**8 ounces bleu cheese, crumbled or cut into small pieces**
**⅛ cup minced white onion**
**¾ cup shelled and finely chopped pecans**

1. Mix together the cream cheese, bleu cheese, and minced onion with a fork until well combined.
2. Form 1-inch balls by gently pressing and shaping between slightly oiled palms. Roll in pecans. Place on waxed paper lined tray, cover, and refrigerate until ready to serve.

**Yields: About 24**

# Asparagus Tips In Pine Nuts

Here's another easy and attractive presentation for large numbers of guests. They are as easy to eat as they are to make, which says they're excellent for passing at a party or on a platter at a finger food buffet. Peppered cream cheese, with the subtle flavor and texture of pine nuts and the crunch of asparagus, makes these not only beautiful but unusually delicious. The leftover stem of the asparagus can be made into soup, or incorporated into a casserole for another meal.

**24 asparagus spikes**
**16 ounces cream cheese, cold**
**2 quarts boiling salted water**
**2 tablespoons cracked pepper**
**½ cup finely chopped pine nuts**

1. Cut tips from asparagus spears in 1½-inch lengths.
2. Form cream cheese into 24 balls and place on waxed paper-lined tray.
3. Place asparagus tips in colander in the sink. Carefully pour boiling salted water over the tips, then immediately run cold water over them to cool. Pat dry and insert asparagus into each ball of cheese, leaving tip exposed.
3. Sprinkle pepper over cheese and carefully roll each ball in the pine nuts. Replace on lined tray, cover, and refrigerate until ready to serve.

**Yields: 24 spikes**

# Chicken Liver Pâté With Cognac, Apple And Truffles

*This spectacular paté is another crowd pleaser. Being very rich, it satisfies a large number of people. The deep, smoky flavor of cognac with the tartness of the apple brings out a richness of the livers that makes this pâté unique. The day after the party it is delicious spread on French bread with some ripe Brie and watercress. Believe me, a sandwich like this would be talked about for several tailgates to come!*

- 2 tablespoons olive oil
- 1 cup minced white onion
- 1 cup sliced mushrooms
- 2 pounds chicken livers, rinsed and drained on paper towel
- ½ cup cognac
- 1 tablespoon salt
- 1 tablespoon cracked pepper
- 1 tablespoon paprika
- 1 cup Granny Smith apples, peeled, cored, and chunked
- 1 pound unsalted butter
- ⅛ cup scant thinly sliced black truffle* (optional)

1. Heat oil in large, heavy, deep skillet over medium-high heat. Add onion and cook until golden. Add mushrooms, stir, and sauté for 1 minute.

*Continued*

---

*Truffles are very expensive and found more commonly canned than fresh. They are of the mushroom family. They grow underground and are found by specially trained pigs and dogs. They are best sliced paper thin; there is a special truffle slicer for this purpose but it is not essential if you have a very sharp knife. They are almost always added at the last moment or used as a garnish.

2. Reduce heat to medium and place livers over the onions in an even layer. Pour cognac over the livers. Cover and cook for 5 minutes over medium-low heat. Uncover, add salt, pepper, and paprika. Stir contents to mix. Turn livers and return heat to medium. Cook uncovered for 5 minutes more.

3. Add apples to pan, reduce heat to low, and cover, cooking 5 more minutes. Remove from heat and allow to stand for 30 minutes.

4. Place contents of pan along with the butter into food processor fitted with steel blade. Pulse about 5 times, scrape down sides, and process until mixture is smooth. Add truffle and pulse once just to mix truffle in.

5. Pour into heavily-oiled 2-quart mold of choice, cover, and refrigerate up to 3 days but at least overnight. Unmold by dipping bottom and two-thirds of sides in hot water for 20 seconds. Cover mold with serving platter and invert, shaking gently if necessary. Garnish with chopped hard-boiled egg and sweet gherkins if desired.

**Serves up to 30 for appetizers**

# Red And White Cabbage Relish

*This is a perfect accompaniment to smoked sliced beef, pork and duck, and most cheeses. It is simple to make and is an attractive addition to any buffet table. Keep it covered in the refrigerator for up to a week.*

> **1 cup finely shredded white cabbage**
> **1 cup finely shredded red cabbage**
> **¼ cup chopped pimiento**
> **¼ cup minced scallions**
> **2 tablespoons poppy seeds**
> **¼ cup red wine vinegar**
> **½ cup water**
> **2 tablespoons granulated sugar**
> **1 teaspoon salt**
> **1 tablespoon cracked pepper**

1. Combine the cabbages, pimiento, scallions and poppy seeds in glass or ceramic bowl.
2. Mix together the vinegar, water, sugar, salt, and pepper and pour over cabbage mixture. Stir to combine, cover, and refrigerate.

**Yields: About ⅔ quart**

# Caviar Egg Salad

*The type of caviar you choose to use here is optional depending on choice and budget. At our restaurant, we used American Golden from sturgeon. Everyone loved it and the cost was relatively low. If a more expensive type, such as Beluga or Sevruga is used, instead of folding it into the egg salad, I suggest serving the egg salad as a canapé garnished with the caviar. This maximizes the texture of the caviar and minimizes breakage of the tender eggs. The selection of caviar is up to you. Our family devours this on toasted wheat bread, open-faced, and topped with watercress leaves.*

**12 eggs**
**¾ cup mayonnaise**
**2 tablespoons prepared mustard**
**4 ounces caviar of your choice**

1. Place eggs in deep sauce pan that has a tight fitting lid. Cover eggs with cool water. Bring to a boil over medium-high heat, cover, and turn off heat. Allow pan to sit covered for 25 minutes. Drain eggs and cover with cold tap water for 5 minutes. Peel shell off eggs. This method of boiling eggs seems to consistently yield beautiful yellow yolks with no darkened outer layers. (Thanks, Mom!)

2. Finely grate the eggs into a glass or ceramic bowl and stir in mayonnaise and mustard. Cover and refrigerate until ready to serve or up to 36 hours in advance.

3. Just before serving, fold caviar into egg salad, being careful not to break the fish eggs.

**Serves 6–8 for lunch or up to 24 for appetizers**

# Italian White Bean Salad

*This is as pleasing mounded atop a crisp green salad as it is served alone or on a buffet table. It was inspired by a version we enjoyed in Florence, but you can enjoy the same flavor without making the trip. Tossed with bacon, garlic and fresh Parmesan with a hint of cracked pepper, this salad will quickly become a favorite. It is easily made and keeps well in the refrigerator in a covered glass bowl for up to a week.*

> 2 cups prepared Italian white beans,* drained
> ¼ cup chopped scallions
> ½ cup bacon, cooked crisp and crumbled
> ½ cup grated Parmesan cheese
> ¼ cup chopped fresh parsley
> ¼ cup olive oil
> 1 tablespoon granulated sugar
> 1 teaspoon minced garlic
> 2 tablespoons red wine vinegar
> 1 tablespoon cracked pepper

1. Place beans, scallions, bacon, Parmesan, and parsley in glass or ceramic bowl.
2. Mix together the oil, sugar, garlic, vinegar, and pepper. Pour over beans and stir. Cover and refrigerate up to 3 days, stirring occasionally.

**Serves 6–8, or up to 16 as appetizers**

---

*
Available at Italian markets.

## Lupini Bean Salad

*The texture of prepared lupini beans (available at Italian markets and in some import sections of good supermarkets) is an experience one should not miss. Some brands are salty and should be rinsed under cold water for a good five minutes to remove the saltiness. If you are invited to someone's house for dinner and you want to bring something besides wine, fill a quart Mason jar with this salad, tie a bow around the rim, and you'll be a hit!*

**2 cups prepared lupini beans, rinsed under cold water for 5 minutes and drained**
**1 cup prepared red lentils, drained**
**½ cup minced red onion**
**½ cup minced, roasted and marinated red peppers***
**¼ cup fresh parsley**
**½ cup grated Parmesan cheese**
**½ cup extra virgin olive oil**
**¼ cup red wine vinegar**
**1 tablespoon fresh lime juice**
**2 tablespoons granulated sugar**
**1 teaspoon minced garlic**
**1 tablespoon cracked pepper**

1. Place beans, lentils, onion, peppers, parsley, and Parmesan in glass or ceramic bowl.
2. Mix together oil, vinegar, lime juice, sugar, garlic, and pepper. Pour over beans, stir, cover, and refrigerate until serving or up to 4 days. Bring to room temperature just before serving for lunch or dinner, but bring to table cold for a cocktail buffet.

**Serves 6–8, or up to 18 for appetizers**

---

* In a jar, or see recipe.

# Caviar Cucumber Salad

*Not only is this pretty on the table, it really tastes remarkably refreshing. For a special picnic, tailgate, or poolside lunch, enjoy inside a pita bread pocket or alongside a piece of cold poached salmon with a glass of Fuisse Sevruga. It is always a success for cocktails, especially with extra dry martinis and brut champagne.*

> **3 firm cucumbers, each about 8 inches long**
> **1 tablespoon fresh lemon juice**
> **¼ cup minced red onion**
> **¼ cup finely crumbled bleu cheese**
> **1 cup sour cream**
> **3 ounces Sevruga caviar**

1. Peel cucumbers and cut in half lengthwise. Scoop out seeds, leaving a trough down the center of each half. Slice across into very thin pieces that will be shaped like crescents. You may use a slicing blade in your food processor or a very sharp knife to achieve thin slices. Place in glass or ceramic bowl and toss with lemon juice.
2. Mix together the onion, bleu cheese, and sour cream. Pour over cucumber slices and mix to cover each slice. Cover and refrigerate up to 24 hours before serving.
3. To serve, place cucumbers in a shallow quiche-type serving dish and sprinkle the caviar over the top. For sandwiches, gently fold caviar directly into cucumbers, being very gentle.

**Serves 6–8, or up to 18 for appetizers**

# Pumpernickel Pizzas

*These are particularly popular, easy to make, and always a party pleaser. They hold well in a warm oven and can be fancied up by adding shredded smoked fowl or pine nuts.*

> ½ cup shredded mozzarella cheese
> ½ cup grated Parmesan cheese
> ½ cup mayonnaise
> 1 tablespoon ketchup
> ¼ cup chopped black olives
> ¼ cup chopped scallions
> ¼ cup chopped pimiento
> 24 slices cocktail-size sliced pumpernickel bread

1. Mix together all ingredients to combine, excluding bread.
2. Divide cheese mixture among bread slices arranged flat on one or two cookie sheets or jelly-roll pans.
3. Place under broiler on middle shelf and broil until browned and bubbly. Serve immediately.

**Yields: 24**

# Creamy Carrot Salad

Here's another refreshing combination that is great poolside or with a piece of smoked trout at a garden luncheon. The creamy base, spiked with scallions and crunchy with almonds, makes this a flavorful way to serve fresh carrots. Surround it with cocktail shrimp for a novel presentation.

> 3 cups grated carrots
> 1 cup slivered almonds
> ½ cup chopped scallions
> ½ cup chopped celery
> 1 cup sour cream
> 1 tablespoon cracked pepper
> 1 teaspoon salt
> 1 teaspoon paprika

1. Mix together all ingredients. Cover and refrigerate.

**Serves 6–8, or up to 18 for appetizers**

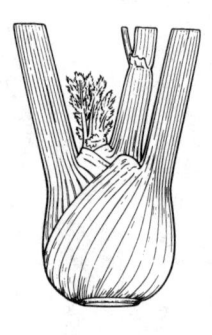

# Spinach Pancakes

*These are not only great served with crème fraîche on a buffet table, but a lovely companion to veal or chicken dishes. Topped with tapenade, caviar, a variety of chutneys, or a mélange of cream cheese and salmon with minced onion, they're heaven. Using frozen spinach elimates the tedious duty of cleaning and blanching fresh.*

**1 cup frozen spinach, thawed, wrung out in a kitchen towel, and chopped**
**½ cup minced onion**
**1 teaspoon salt**
**1 teaspoon cracked pepper**
**1 cup breadcrumbs**
**3 eggs, slightly beaten**
**1 tablespoon cream**
**4 tablespoons butter for frying**

1. Mix together all ingredients except butter.
2. Heat 1 tablespoon butter in heavy nonstick skillet over medium-high heat. Using a tablespoon, drop in spinach batter to form 6 small pancakes. Brown on each side and remove to tray in warm oven. Repeat, making three more batches for approximately 24 cocktail size pancakes.

**Yields: 24 pancakes**
**Serves 4**

# Potato Pancakes

Here's the ultimate treat when served with sour cream laced with onions and generous supplies of caviar. This recipe works just as well when served with apple sauce at a latke party. What is a latke, you say? A latke is a pancake made in the Jewish tradition for Channukah. Spiked with onion, they are heavenly served beside beef brisket, stuffed cabbage or a dish of applesauce. My mother's were more hash-brown style but many people make them from mashed or baked potatoes.

- 2 cups warm potatoes, mashed, or baked and peeled
- ½ cup chopped scallions with greens
- ¼ cup unsalted butter, melted
- 1 tablespoon salt, or to taste
- 1 tablespoon cracked pepper
- 4 eggs, slightly beaten
- 1 cup breadcrumbs
- 8 tablespoons butter or margarine for frying

1. In a glass or ceramic bowl using a fork, whip the potatoes, scallions, melted butter, salt, pepper, and eggs until light and well-blended.

2. Spread one-half of the breadcrumbs in an even layer on waxed paper. With a tablespoon, dollop the potato mixture into 24 mounds on the crumbs. Gently press into ¾-inch thick patties. Sprinkle the remaining breadcrumbs over each patty and gently press crumbs into surface.

3. Heat 2 tablespoons of the butter for frying in large, heavy skillet over medium-high heat until foam subsides. Fry 6 pancakes at a time, browning both sides of each patty. Hold in tray in warm oven until ready to serve but no more than a few hours.

**Yields: 24 cocktail-size pancakes**

## Buckwheat Blinis

*These blinis are ahhh-inspiring with caviar, tapenade, smoked salmon, or simply a small dollop of sour cream garnished with chives. They are especially handsome presented on a silver tray lined with a damask napkin folded into a diamond shape.*

> 1 ¼-ounce envelope active dry yeast
> 1 cup milk, scalded and cooled to 115 degrees
> ¾ cup buckwheat flour
> ¾ cup unbleached all-purpose flour
> 2 tablespoons unsalted butter, melted
> 1 teaspoon salt
> 1 teaspoon cracked pepper
> 4 eggs, slightly beaten
> 8 tablespoons butter or margarine for frying

1. Dissolve yeast in warm scalded milk in glass bowl and stir in the buckwheat flour. Allow to stand in a warm, draft-free spot such as an oven which was turned on for 60 seconds and then turned off. (Do not set bowl directly on rack of oven, but on folded towel or hotpad.)
2. Stir in the unbleached flour, melted butter, salt, cracked pepper, and eggs. Allow to stand 15 more minutes in warm, draft-free place.
3. Heat 2 tablespoons of the butter for frying in heavy, nonstick skillet over medium-high heat until foam subsides. Using a tablespoon, drop 6 dollops into pan to form 6 3-inch pancakes. Brown on both sides. Hold in warm oven. Repeat for three more batches. Serve warm. To hold more than 30 minutes, cover with foil for up to 2 hours.

**Yields: 24 cocktail-size pancakes**

# Whole Beef Tenderloin With Raspberry Sauce

Here's a striking presentation for a cocktail buffet. The pink sauce, with a base of raspberries, served alongside the toasted onion-crusted beef is like a picture from a magazine. Slice and place in mini French rolls halved lengthwise. It works well cold for a luncheon or tailgate party. You'll love the flavor-enhancing qualities of the raspberry sauce.

## Beef

- ½ cup unsalted butter, softened
- ½ cup minced white onion
- 1 tablespoon salt
- 1 tablespoon cracked pepper
- 1 4- to 5-pound whole beef tenderloin, trimmed and tied by butcher

1. Combine the butter, onion, salt and pepper. Place tenderloin on roasting tray and coat with onion-butter mixture.
2. Place beef in preheated 500-degree F. oven for 20 minutes. Reduce heat to 325 degrees and roast an additional 20 minutes for rare, or 30 minutes for medium. (You may test for desired doneness with a meat thermometer if unsure.)
3. Make sauce while roasting beef.

## Sauce

- ½ pound bacon, minced
- ½ cup minced white onion
- 1 cup heavy cream
- 2 cups fresh raspberries, rinsed and drained on paper towel

*Continued*

1. Place the bacon in heavy, deep saucepan over medium-high heat and cook until the bacon browns. Add onion and cook mixture until onion browns. Pour off any excess fat. Let cool for 10 minutes.
2. Place mixture in food processor fitted with steel blade. Pulse to combine, then pour in cream and raspberries, reserving ¼ cup of the most perfect berries for garnish. Pulse to blend contents into a thick sauce, scraping sides of bowl as needed.

## To Serve

3. Coat a serving platter with half of the sauce, saving the balance to serve on the side. Slice the beef and arrange on the sauce. Dot with the remaining fresh berries and serve hot, warm, or cold.

**Serves 6–8, or up to 24 for appetizers (carve thinly to serve more guests)**

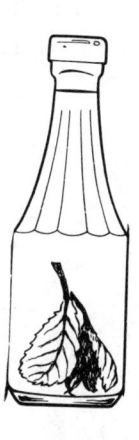

# Toasted Onion Chicken

*This simple way to make chicken inspires rave reviews. Cut the chicken breast halves into smaller pieces for appetizers. A little hoisin sauce (available in the Oriental section of most supermarkets) makes a superior dipping sauce and colors the center of your platter. Stuff inside a French roll with mayonnaise and Dijon and you are on your way to a fabulous picnic.*

> 1 cup butter, softened
> ½ cup minced white onion
> 1 tablespoon salt
> 1 tablespoon cracked pepper
> 6 small boneless chicken breasts[*]

1. Mix together the butter, onion, salt, and pepper and coat each piece of chicken.
2. Place chicken on roasting tray and put in preheated 350-degree F. oven for about 20 to 25 minutes or until chicken juices run clear and skin is crisp and almost brown. For a cocktail buffet, divide the halves again for 24 pieces. You may also serve them cut into chunks and skewered with the end of a wooden toothpick for dipping.

**Serves 6**

---

[*] They are often sold halved, in which case get 12. If not, have the butcher cut them in half to end up with 12 boneless chicken breast halves.

# American Foo Young

This is a popular carryover from my years at Grinnell College. My friends from New York would show up at my apartment at 11:30 p.m. craving Chinese food. I was always able to appease these students by creating this dish with ingredients already in my refrigerator.

- **6 eggs, slightly beaten**
- **1 tablespoon soy sauce**
- **2 cups fresh bean sprouts, rinsed and drained on paper towel**
- **½ cup chopped scallions with greens**
- **½ cup chopped celery**
- **½ cup watercress leaves, rinsed and drained**
- **½ cup safflower oil, or other light oil for frying**

1. Mix together the eggs and soy sauce.
2. Place bean sprouts, scallions, celery, and watercress in a bowl and pour egg mixture over. Stir gently to combine.
3. Heat ¼ cup of the oil in a large, heavy sauté or fry pan over high heat until oil is very hot but not smoking. Using a tablespoon, drop in dollops of the mixture to form 6 small pancakes. Reduce heat to medium-high and brown on both sides.
4. Remove patties to tray in warm oven while frying two more batches, adding one-half of the remaining oil before each batch. Serve hot.

**Yields: About 18 cocktail size pancakes**

# Blueberry Rhubarb Chutney

*I created this chutney in Maine when the blueberries were at their peak. Maine berries are a bit smaller than those grown elsewhere and oh, so sweet! This is a dessert chutney, to be served with a tray of sponge cake or pound cake and it's spectacular on any dessert table. We usually put the sweets at a separate location for a cocktail buffet in order to divert guests to another area. There, we like to create a more luxurious setting for the presentation by surrounding the desserts with flowers and silver serving pieces.*

- **2 cups rhubarb stalks, trimmed and sliced into 1-inch pieces**
- **⅛ cup grated lemon rind**
- **2 cups granulated sugar**
- **⅛ cup water**
- **2 cups fresh blueberries, picked over for stems, rinsed, and drained**
- **1 tablespoon ground cinnamon**

1. Place rhubarb, lemon rind, sugar, and water in a heavy saucepan and heat over medium-high heat until sugar melts and mixture begins to bubble, occasionally stirring gently. Reduce heat to medium-low and boil for 15 minutes, watching to prevent a boil over.
2. Add blueberries and cinnamon to pan and stir until contents begin to boil once more, raising heat if necessary. Boil 5 more minutes. Remove from heat and cool 30 minutes. Pour into glass bowl, cover, and refrigerate up to 4 days.

**Yields: About 1 quart**

# Stuffed Dipped Apricots

*Even a child can make these — and they have fun doing it. At my house we make them a lot. They keep for at least a week; that is if someone doesn't raid the fridge. Neufchatel cheese originated in the small Normandy town bearing its name. Soft and white and tasting lke cream cheese, it is lower in fat and readily found flavored with fruits or herbs.*

**¾ cup mandarin- or strawberry-flavored Neufchatel cheese, softened**
**24 large, whole dried apricots, pitted**
**½ cup melted dipping chocolate**

1. Place the cheese in a small pastry bag fitted with a small-ended tip.
2. "Stuff" each apricot with cheese by gently filling through the hole where the pit was removed.
3. Dip two-thirds of each stuffed apricot in melted chocolate, leaving a bit of the cheese showing at the exposed end. Place on waxed paper to harden. Cover and refrigerate until ready to serve.

**Yields: 24 apricots**

# Cold Stuffed Lobster Tails

*As a child I remember my parents throwing a fabulous party where, in the entrance hall, a children's wading pool was placed on a small round table, draped, and filled with a mountain of shaved ice. Arranged on the ice were stuffed lobster tails, stone crab claws, and cocktail shrimp. What a presentation! I have not forgotten that mountain of delicacies to this day.*

**12 small lobster tails, 4 to 6 ounces each, split all the way down the middle, veins removed (this can be done by your fish purveyor)**
**1 cup water**
**¾ cup mayonnaise**
**1 tablespoon prepared mustard**
**1 tablespoon celery seed**
**1 teaspoon fresh lemon juice**

1. Place the split lobster tails shell side down in a roasting pan. Pour in the water and cover pan tightly with foil.
2. Place the pan in a preheated 350-degree F. oven for about 15 minutes or until lobster meat is just cooked. (You may check once, toward the end of cooking time, keeping face away when lifting foil to avoid steam. Reseal to cook further.)
3. Remove from oven and allow to cool.
4. Remove meat from shells, being careful not to break the shells. Rinse shells, place in sealed plastic bag, and refrigerate.
5. Chop lobster meat and toss with mayonnaise, mustard, celery seed, and lemon juice. Cover and chill up to 24 hours before serving.
6. Divide lobster salad among tail shell halves and arrange on a beautiful platter (or a huge mountain of shaved ice!).

**Yields: 24 appetizers**

# Clam Stuffed Chicken Breasts

*While I do not actually slit and stuff the breasts, the method by which this is done makes it appear as if the breast is stuffed. The combination of shellfish and fowl, enhanced by garlic and herbs under smooth, bubbly cheese, creates a savory blend of tastes. This marvelous and flavorful combination is an attractive presentation at a buffet.*

**3 eggs, slightly beaten**
**3 tablespoons dry sherry**
**8 large chicken breast halves, skinned and boned**
**2 cups breadcrumbs**
**¼ cup olive oil**
**1 teaspoon minced garlic**
**½ cup butter**
**1 cup minced onion**
**1 cup tomato purée**
**1 teaspoon salt**
**1 tablespoon cracked pepper**
**1 teaspoon dried oregano**
**1 cup dry red wine**
**½ cup unsalted butter**
**1 teaspoon minced garlic**
**½ cup minced shallots**
**2 cups clams, drained**
**1 cup breadcrumbs**
**1 cup shredded fontina cheese**
**½ cup grated Parmesan cheese**

1. Mix together eggs and sherry and allow chicken to soak in the mixture for 30 minutes. Dredge in breadcrumbs to coat.
2. Heat oil with garlic in large, heavy sauté pan over medium-high heat and brown both sides of chicken. Arrange on baking sheet with sides.

*Continued*

3. In same unwashed sauté pan over medium-high heat, add ½ cup butter and onion. Sauté for 5 minutes. Stir in tomato purée, salt, pepper, and oregano and reduce heat to medium-low. Stir in wine. Simmer for 2 minutes and pour over chicken.
4. Heat ½ cup butter in sauté pan with garlic and shallots over medium-high heat, stirring occasionally until shallots begin to turn golden. Turn off heat and stir in clams and breadcrumbs. Divide among chicken in mounds.
5. Sprinkle fontina over the chicken and Parmesan over that.
6. Place in preheated 350-degree F. oven for 30 minutes or until cheese is brown and bubbly.

**Serves 6–8**

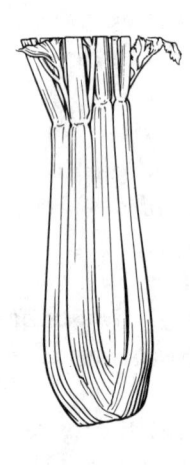

# Stuffed Sirloin Roll

*This a real meat and potatoes dish all in one. Almost like meatloaf-encased mashed potatoes, the addition of scallions and cheddar cheese makes this a family pleasing dish that is easily assembled and refrigerated for baking just before serving.*

**2 pounds ground sirloin**
**3 eggs, slightly beaten**
**1 cup breadcrumbs**
**1 cup minced red onion**
**1 tablespoon Worcestershire sauce**
**1 tablespoon cracked pepper**
**1 tablespoon soy sauce**
**2 cups mashed potatoes**
**½ cup chopped scallions**
**1 cup sour cream**
**½ cup shredded mild cheddar cheese**

1. Mix together the sirloin, eggs, breadcrumbs, onion, Worcestershire, pepper, and soy sauce and spread into 1-inch thick rectangle on plastic wrap.
2. Mix together the potatoes, scallion, sour cream, and cheddar cheese. Spread in even layer over sirloin leaving an inch uncovered on the long side at the top.
3. Starting at the bottom, roll up as you would a jelly-roll, using the plastic wrap for help, until the 1-inch strip meets sirloin and the filling is enclosed except for the ends.
4. Carefully place roll on baking sheet with sides and place in preheated 325-degree F. oven for 90 minutes.

**Serves 6–8**

# Herbed Scallops With Smoked Salmon

This delicate combination is excellent over rice or pasta. Or serve it as an appetizer in a chafing dish on a buffet table for rave reviews. With white wine or dry champagne it makes for a decadent midnight snack.

> **2 pounds sea scallops**
> **¼ cup all-purpose flour**
> **½ cup unsalted butter**
> **1 tablespoon olive oil**
> **⅛ cup minced shallots**
> **½ cup chopped parsley**
> **1 teaspoon salt**
> **1 tablespoon cracked pepper**
> **¼ cup dry sherry**
> **1 teaspoon fresh lemon juice**
> **1 teaspoon dill weed**
> **½ pound smoked Nova or Scottish salmon, cut into 2-inch strips**

1. Cut scallops across the grain into discs about ½-inch thick and toss with flour to coat.
2. Heat butter, olive oil, and shallots in heavy sauté pan over medium-high heat and sauté for 2 minutes. Stir in parsley and stir for 1 minute more. Reduce heat to medium and stir in salt, pepper, sherry, lemon juice, and dill. Stir for 1 minute. Add scallops, cover, and reduce heat to low for 3 minutes.
3. Remove pan from heat, stir in salmon, and serve immediately.

**Serves 6–8 for supper or up to 18 as an appetizer**

# Basil Cream Sauce

*This is a delectable sauce for pasta, poached fish or chicken, and just about any steamed vegetable. It is very rich and simple to make. Try it over the Stuffed Sirloin Roll or the Chicken Liver Omelette.*

> ½ cup unsalted butter
> 1 teaspoon minced garlic
> 1 cup minced onion
> ½ cup chopped parsley
> 1 cup chopped fresh basil
> 1 teaspoon salt
> 1 tablespoon cracked pepper
> 1 tablespoon all-purpose flour
> ½ cup dry white wine
> 1½ cups heavy cream

1. Heat butter in heavy sauce pan over medium-high heat and stir in garlic and onion. Sauté for 5 minutes. Stir in parsley and sauté 1 minute more. Reduce heat to medium and stir in basil, salt, and pepper.
2. Sprinkle flour over the top and stir for 2 minutes. Stir in white wine.
3. Gradually stir in cream and continue stirring until sauce thickens. Serve immediately.

**Yields: About 2 cups**

# Chicken Liver Omelette

An elegant brunch or late supper, this makes a handsome presentation. Cooking the livers in this way gives them a light crust which adds not only taste, but texture, to the savory filling.

**2 cups all-purpose flour**
**2 tablespoons salt**
**2 tablespoons cracked pepper**
**2 tablespoons dried basil**
**2 tablespoons dried parsley**
**2 pounds fresh chicken livers, rinsed and drained on paper towels**
**⅓ cup olive oil**
**1 cup sliced onion**
**½ cup unsalted butter**
**12 eggs, lightly beaten**
**1 teaspoon salt**
**½ cup grated Parmesan cheese**

1. Mix together flour, salt, pepper, basil, and parsley in a large zipper-lock plastic bag.
2. Place livers in bag and seal the bag, enclosing as much air as possible. Shake bag to coat livers heavily.
3. Heat oil in large, heavy skillet over medium-high heat and stir in onion. Sauté onion for 4 minutes. Arrange livers over onion and brown both sides for 8 minutes each. Turn pan to low heat and make omelette.
4. Heat butter in large omelette pan over medium-high heat. Beat eggs and salt together until slightly frothy. When foam subsides on butter, add eggs and stir pan gently and slowly for about 1 minute. Bring sides of cooked egg to center and tip pan to coat sides with raw egg from pan's center. Cook over medium heat until center is almost firm. Sprinkle with Parmesan.
5. Arrange livers over one-half of the omelette and flip the other half over to cover. Serve immediately.

**Serves 6–8**

## Crêpes And Variations

Crêpes are a favorite dish because of their convenience and versatility. Crêpes are a French term for a pancake of ultra thinness. The ingredients for basic crêpes are almost always on hand, making it easy to whip up a delicious lunch or snack with no notice. And these slim pancakes can be filled with all sorts of good things from shredded ham and melted cheese to fresh fruit. Add a tablespoon of sugar to the batter if using a sweet filling.

    3 eggs
    1 egg yolk
    1¼ cups milk
    1 cup all-purpose flour
    ½ teaspoon salt
    1 teaspoon unsalted butter, melted
    ⅛ unsalted butter for frying

1. Mix together eggs, yolk, and milk until combined. Stir in flour and salt until most of the lumps are gone (some small lumps give character). Stir in the melted butter.
2. Heat 1 tablespoon of butter in a crêpe pan or small omelette pan over medium-high heat until foam subsides. Ladle in a small amount of batter, swirl the pan to coat, and pour excess batter back into bowl. Replace pan over heat until crepe browns. Flip onto towel and repeat with all batter.
3. Place filling on uncooked side of crêpe and roll up. Filling suggestions: chopped chicken or turkey, chopped brisket with minced scallions, any cheese, cut up fruit, sautéed vegetables, fresh crab in melted cheddar, shrimp in garlic butter, smoked salmon mixed with onion and cream cheese, herring in cream sauce, and toasted onion sour cream.

**Yields: About 36**

## Poached Pears And Variations

*I make these for people on sugar-restricted diets, as there is no added fat or sugar. This is not true once you drizzle on melted chocolate and serve on chantilly cream, but they are fine unadorned. Since they are poached in champagne, they are perfect for a special occasion or New Year's Eve.*

**8 Bosc pears, well-shaped with strong stems**
**2 cups champagne**
**1 cinnamon stick**
**8 cloves**

1. Peel pears and trim bottoms so they stand solidly. Arrange in deep baking dish with cover.
2. Pour champagne over pears and place cinnamon stick in liquid. Stick a clove in each pear. Cover tightly.
3. Place dish in preheated 350-degree F. oven for 60 minutes or until pears are tender. Serve warm or chilled.
4. For variation: drizzle with white or dark melted chocolate and serve on sweetened whipped cream topped with nuts or coconut; serve warm with thawed frozen raspberries in syrup; serve beside a fudgy brownie with ice cream; or top with warmed apricot preserves.

**Serves 8**

*Chapter V*

# SOUP, PASTA AND ONE DISH MEALS

Sometimes less is better. There are many occasions when a complex soup, a crusty roll, and a bottle of wine make a perfectly balanced meal. Imagine a brisk Sunday afternoon with friends coming over to watch a movie. Consider a meal of Black Bean soup, Cheddar Jalapeño Muffins and Molasses Crisps, all of which can be made the day before. This satisfying menu is not only delicious, but allows the hosts to completely relax and enjoy the afternoon (and the movie). This is what entertaining is all about.

Lobster soup and a crusty roll with a bottle of light beer make for a luxurious early supper, complete and satisfying. For an added treat, you may want to prepare some poached pears the day before to sweetly refresh the palate after enjoying the soup. Using your imagination, you can entertain beautifully and easily with a minimal amount of cleanup. Soon you will find yourself preferring home and "easygoing entertaining."

For a casual place setting enhancement, purchase large white paper napkins, open them and gather them attractively in the center, and stuff them into a champagne flue. For a festive feeling, sprinkle metallic confetti found at party supply stores over a white paper cloth. Mix juice with sparkling water for an alcohol-free toast. The simple and creative touches will set the mood for a casual one-dish meal. Enjoy!

*Chapter V*

# SOUP, PASTA AND ONE DISH MEALS
## Recipe List

*Fried Soufflé*
*Crabmeat and Asparagus Soup*
*Lobster Soup*
*Black Bean Soup*
*Three Onion Soup Gratinée*
*Three Onion Panade*
*Potato Soup*
*Hearty Vegetable Soup*
*Sherried Clam Chowder*
*Spinach Soup*
*Chicken Stock*
*Cucumber Soup*
*Basic Pasta Dough with Variations*
*Caesar Pasta Salad*
*Pasta with Walnuts, Garlic and Butter*
*Angel Hair Pasta in Pink Tomato Sauce*
*Pasta Alfredo*
*Pasta Carbonara*
*Pasta Stuffed Peppers*
*Veal Sauce*
*Scalloped Potatoes with Ham*
*Shrimp and Scallop Jambalaya*

# Fried Soufflé

*Here's a quick yet elegant brunch for friends or family. It is delicious unadorned, but can be served with a topping such as sautéed mushrooms or even crab. This is a light and airy egg dish with a touch of Parmesan browned on the top for a crispy topping. We enjoy having out-of-town friends stay with us, and this recipe is invaluable for mornings when we prefer to spend our time relaxing and chatting rather than cooking.*

**12 eggs, separated**
**1 cup grated Parmesan cheese**
**½ cup plain breadcrumbs**
**1 teaspoon salt**
**1 tablespoon cracked pepper, or to taste**
**1 teaspoon cream of tartar**
**⅛ cup unsalted butter**

1. Mix together the egg yolks, Parmesan, breadcrumbs, salt, and pepper.
2. In another bowl, beat the egg whites with cream of tartar until stiff peaks are formed when the beaters are lifted.
3. Heat butter in 12-inch nonstick ovenproof omelette or sauté pan over medium-high heat.
4. Quickly fold one-fourth of the whipped egg whites into the egg yolk mixture. Then gently fold the yolk mixture into the egg whites and pour into the hot buttered pan. Fry for 3 minutes. Place pan in preheated oven on highest setting. Bake for 5 minutes for a soft texture or up to 8 minutes for a firmer texture.

**Serves 6–8**

# Crabmeat And Asparagus Soup

*Served with crusty rolls and a little butter, this delicious potage makes an appetizing lunch or late supper. For variety, substitute shredded carrots for the asparagus, and poached white fish for the crab. You may want to offer chow mein noodles and toasted sesame seeds as a garnish, since this soup was inspired by a Chinese dish.*

- **6 cups chicken stock (see page 159)**
- **2 eggs, slightly beaten**
- **2 tablespoons cornstarch**
- **¼ cup dry sherry**
- **1 tablespoon soy sauce**
- **1 teaspoon sesame oil**
- **1 teaspoon cracked pepper**
- **2 cups asparagus, trimmed and cut into one-inch pieces**
- **3 cups boiling water**
- **1 cup crabmeat, rinsed, drained and picked over for shell**

1. Bring stock to a simmer over medium-high heat. Slowly pour in egg in a stream while stirring soup to form egg "feathers." Reduce heat to medium-low to stop simmer.
2. Mix together corn starch, sherry, soy sauce, sesame oil, and pepper until smooth. Slowly stir into soup and continue to stir until soup begins to thicken. Raise heat a bit if necessary, but reduce it again as soon as soup thickens.
3. Place asparagus in a colander in the sink and pour the boiling water over the pieces. Place pieces in soup along with crabmeat and serve as soon as crab is hot, about 60 seconds.

**Serves 6–8**

# Lobster Soup

*Spending many summers on the coast of Maine allowed us the luxury of cooking and eating fresh, delicious lobster as often as we wished. A fisherman named Sonny lived just a few miles down the "neck" from our home, and we would call him in the morning to order lobsters and crab for that evening. Sonny would catch the shellfish, then keep the live lobsters in sea water until we picked them up while his wife boiled up the crab and picked out the meat. Talk about heaven on earth! Who needs meat when lobster is just $2.99 a pound?*

- ¼ cup butter or margarine
- ½ cup minced onion
- 1 cup sliced mushrooms
- ¼ cup minced fresh parsley
- ½ teaspoon minced garlic
- 1 tablespoon cracked pepper
- 1 teaspoon salt
- 2 tablespoons all-purpose flour
- 2½ cups whole milk or 1½ cups milk and 1 cup cream for richer soup
- ¼ cup tomato purée
- 1½ cups cooked lobster meat, cut into chunks
- Oyster crackers or crusty French bread to serve with soup

1. In a deep, heavy pot heat the butter over medium-high heat until foam subsides. Add onion, mushrooms, parsley, garlic, pepper, and salt to pan and stir 4 to 5 minutes.
2. Reduce heat to medium and sprinkle flour over the top of the contents of the pan, stirring and cooking for 2 minutes longer. Slowly stir in milk and tomato purée and cook while stirring until soup thickens.
3. Stir lobster meat into soup and cook 2 minutes more. Serve hot with oyster crackers and/or crusty French bread with butter.

**Serves 6–8**

# Black Bean Soup

You will be amazed by the number of people who claim this as their favorite soup. To them I say "Olé!" With sliced grilled chicken over top, it's a complete meal. Garnishes may include sour cream, shredded imported cheddar, chopped red onion, sliced jalapeño peppers, and shredded lettuce. Try it with a jigger of sherry or a shot of tequila. Stand back!

½ pound bacon, minced
1 cup minced white onion
⅛ cup minced jalapeño peppers, seeded*
1 tablespoon minced garlic
½ cup chopped fresh cilantro
3 tablespoons mild chili powder
3 tablespoons ground cumin
12 ounces dried black beans, rinsed and picked over
8 cups water

1. In a large heavy soup pot, cook bacon over medium-high heat until it begins to crisp. Stir in onion, jalapeños, garlic, cilantro, chili powder, and cumin. Cook while stirring for 3 minutes and reduce heat to medium-low. Stir beans into pot and pour in water. Mix well and cover.

2. Cook over medium-low heat for 3 to 4 hours or until beans are tender and liquid is absorbed. Stir to create a thick soup as the beans mush. Serve hot with garnishes.

**Serves 6–8 for a meal or up to 12 as a soup course**

---

* **Always** wear rubber gloves when handling any hot peppers!!!

# Three-Onion Soup Gratinée

*I could eat this every day. Honest. The combination of sherry, buttered cooked onions, and melted cheese is as close to heaven as we may ever get. If you like, serve this with a hot sandwich or a slice of grilled meat or fish. But it is so thick and cheesy, it makes a great meal by itself.*

½ cup unsalted butter or margarine
2 cups sliced white onion
2 cups leeks, sliced into small pieces
½ cup minced shallots
1 teaspoon salt
1 tablespoon cracked pepper
1 teaspoon paprika
½ teaspoon saffron[*]
1 cup dry sherry
2 cups chicken[**] or vegetable stock
6 slices day-old French bread
1 cup grated Parmesan cheese
6 thin slices fontina cheese
6 thin slices mozzarella cheese

1. Heat butter in heavy soup pot over medium-high heat until foam subsides. Stir in onions, leeks, shallots, salt, pepper, paprika, and saffron. Cook while stirring for 5 to 7 minutes or onions are tender.
2. Reduce heat to medium and stir in sherry. Simmer for a minute or two and stir in stock. Remove from heat.

*Continued*

---

[*] Squeeze between thumb and index finger to disperse.

[**] See page 159.

3. Divide soup among 6 ovenproof individual soup crocks. Place a piece of bread on top of soup. Divide Parmesan among crocks on top of bread, then the fontina, and finally the mozzarella.
4. Bake crocks on a tray in hot oven or run under broiler until cheese bubbles and browns.

**Serves 6**

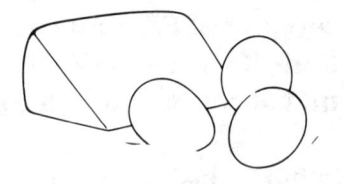

# Three Onion Panade

We made this for a "whim" at our restaurant and had requests for years. It is like French onion soup, but it is served in a casserole and you eat it with a fork. The word "panade" originates from the French word for bread, "pain." In this casserole, French bread is sliced and covered with a blend of onions, leeks and garlic laced with dry sherry and then topped with cheese. Serve it alongside grilled meat or fish, and add a salad and a glass of good wine for a hearty meal which will satisfy everyone.

- 1 cup unsalted butter
- 3 cups thinly sliced white onion
- 2 cups leeks, trimmed and sliced into small pieces
- 1 tablespoon minced garlic
- 1 tablespoon salt, or to taste
- 2 tablespoons cracked pepper
- 1 cup dry sherry
- 1 cup chicken* or vegetable stock
- 1 day old baguette, or other crusty hard bread, sliced in 2-inch slices and left out to air for a few hours
- 2 cups shredded fontina cheese
- 1 cup shredded Parmesan cheese
- 2 tablespoons unsalted butter, melted

1. Heat 1 cup butter in heavy soup pot over medium-high heat until foam subsides. Stir in onion, leeks, garlic, salt, and pepper and stir for 1 minute.

*Continued*

---

\* See page 159.

2. Reduce heat to medium and pour in sherry. Reduce heat to medium-low and cover onions loosely with a piece of foil laid directly onto the onions. Allow to simmer slowly, or "sweat," for 1 hour. Stir in stock and turn off heat.
3. Arrange bread slices in single layer on bottom of generously-buttered 10" x 14" ovenproof, deep casserole dish. The size of the pan may vary a few inches without hurting this recipe.
4. Ladle soup over bread and top with fontina, then the Parmesan. Sprinkle the melted butter over the Parmesan and place in preheated 350-degree F. oven and bake for about an hour, or until the cheese is brown and bubbly. (Just reading this makes me hungry!)

**Serves 8**

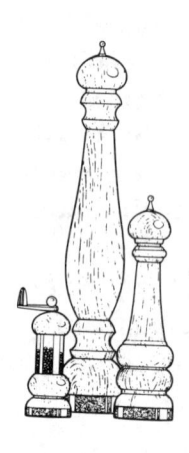

# Potato Soup

*This soup is so smooth and rich, it is exceptionally comforting on a cold stormy night. That's the time to throw caution to the wind and put a pat of butter and a tablespoon of cream on the top of each piping hot bowl. Otherwise, you can chill it and put it in a food processor along with one cup of cream and a handful of chives for incredible vichyssoise.*

> ½ cup unsalted butter
> ½ cup finely grated carrots
> 1 tablespoon minced onion
> 2 teaspoons salt, or to taste
> 1 teaspoon cracked pepper
> 2½ cups flesh from baked and cooled potatoes
> 1 cup heavy cream*
> 1 cup milk

1. Heat butter in a heavy soup kettle over medium-high heat until foam subsides. Add carrot, onion, salt, and pepper and cook for 2 minutes stirring frequently.
2. Stir in potato, reduce heat to medium-low, and gradually pour in cream and/or milk. Heat while stirring until soup is hot and smooth. A few lumps will give this soup character!

**Serves 6–8**

---

* You may omit the cream and double the milk for fewer calories.

# Hearty Vegetable Soup

We served this at a fundraiser that we named "Autumn Country Supper." This blend of garden vegetables with a hint of pepper and oregano and a slightly tomato base is delicious. It's hearty, delectable, and good for you, too!

¼ cup safflower oil, or other light oil
1 cup leeks, cut into small pieces
¼ cup chopped shallots
½ cup chopped fresh parsley
2 tablespoons cracked pepper
1 tablespoon salt, or to taste
1 teaspoon dried oregano
1 cup diced carrots
2 cups peeled, diced potatoes
1 cup broccoli, cut into small flowerettes
1 cup cauliflower, cut into small flowerettes
2 cups chicken[*] or vegetable stock
1 cup frozen yellow corn kernels
1 cup tomato purée
½ cup breadcrumbs

1. Heat oil in heavy soup pot over medium-high heat for 2 minutes. Add leeks, shallots, parsley, pepper, salt, oregano, and carrots. Stir and cook for 2 minutes.
2. Reduce heat to medium and stir in potato, broccoli, and cauliflower and cover for 2 minutes.
3. Stir in stock, corn, and tomato purée and reduce heat to low. Simmer soup, stirring frequently, for 45 minutes.
4. Stir in breadcrumbs and continue to stir over low heat until soup thickens, about 3 minutes. Serve hot.

**Serves 6–8**

---

[*] See page 159.

**Artistic Surroundings**

**Great Pasta**

Fiddlehead Fern Saute'

The Influence of the Orient

**Grilled Lobster and Fresh Corn**

**Sticky Buns**

**The Influence of the Southwest**

Fresh Raspberry Muffins

# Sherried Clam Chowder

Here's another treasure that I came up with one fall evening in the kitchen in Maine. A bowl of this, a crusty roll, and some blueberry cobbler was the perfect prelude to a good night's sleep wrapped in a warm quilt, with the sound of the ocean crashing on the rocks beneath the open window. It must be time to plan another trip.

**2 cups peeled, diced potatoes**
**½ cup unsalted butter**
**¼ cup minced onion**
**¼ cup finely grated carrots**
**¼ cup minced fresh parsley**
**2 teaspoons salt, or to taste**
**1 tablespoon cracked pepper**
**⅛ cup dry sherry**
**1 cup milk**
**2 cups shucked and coarsely chopped clams**
**1 cup heavy cream**

1. Place potato in heavy saucepan with lid and cover with water. Bring to a simmer over medium heat and simmer until potato is firm but cooked; about 15 minutes should do it. Cover and remove from heat.
2. Heat butter in heavy soup pot over medium-high heat until foam subsides. Add onion, carrot, parsley, salt, and pepper to pot and stir for 3 minutes. Stir in sherry and reduce heat to low.
3. Place one-half of the boiled potato, drained, into a food processor fitted with a steel blade. Add the milk and process until smooth. Add to pot.
4. Stir in clams and increase heat to medium. When contents begin to simmer, reduce heat to low and stir in cream. Serve hot.

**Serves 6–8**

# Spinach Soup

*You want a creamy soup with complex, vivacious flavor? Then try this! This delicious creamy soup has a flavor made more provocative by the addition of Romano cheese. Have a glass of dry sherry along with it, and enjoy!*

- ½ cup unsalted butter
- ½ cup minced onion
- ¼ cup chopped fresh parsley
- 1 tablespoon cracked pepper
- 1 teaspoon salt, or to taste
- ¼ cup dry white wine
- 2 cups frozen spinach, thawed and wrung out in a towel, chopped
- 2 tablespoons all-purpose flour
- 2 cups whole milk or 1 cup milk and 1 cup cream
- 1 cup grated Romano cheese

1. Heat butter in heavy soup pot over medium-high heat until foam subsides. Add onion, parsley, pepper, and salt and sauté mixture for 5 minutes. Stir in wine. Add spinach and sauté for 1 minute.

2. Sprinkle flour over mixture and stir for 2 minutes more. Gradually add milk and reduce heat to medium, continuing to stir. When soup thickens, stir in one-half of the cheese. To serve, ladle into hot bowl and top with a small mound of the remaining Romano cheese.

**Serves 6–8**

# Chicken Stock

*This is just like Grandma makes. I always use chicken breasts and make a chicken salad out of them after they are removed from the pot and cooled. A friend of mine insisted that I try throwing a turnip in the pot and I have done so now for years. My daughter considers the cooked turnip the best part of the whole experience.*

> **4 whole chicken breasts**
> **2 carrots**
> **2 stalks celery**
> **1 large white onion**
> **1 large turnip**
> **3 tablespoons coarse salt***
> **1 bay leaf tied with a small bunch of parsley, using kitchen twine (Bouquet Garni)**
> **1½ gallons water**

1. Place all ingredients in a large stock pot and bring to boil over medium-high heat.
2. Reduce heat to medium and simmer for 90 minutes, skimming the foam as it gathers on top.
3. Remove chicken and reserve for another use. Eat or discard the vegetables and discard the parsley/bay leaf bundle. Pour stock through a cheese cloth into a large glass bowl.
4. Cover and refrigerate until fat hardens on top of stock. Remove fat with a spoon. Stock freezes beautifully in zipper-lock plastic bags. (I put 2 cups to a bag so I can use it as needed.)

**Yields: About 1 gallon**

---

* Kosher, available at most supermarkets.

## Cucumber Soup

*I invented this recipe for a friend who requested low or no fat. We served it in champagne flutes with a piece of matzo for garnish. Flavored with curry and cumin, it is rich in flavor and texture, but because non-fat yogurt is used, it contains no fat. You do not necessarily need to mention that fact until after it has been tasted by guests! It also makes a great side dish for grilled meats and fish, or just about any Indian dish. Stuff what is left over into a pita for lunch the next day.*

- 1½ cups plain non-fat yogurt
- 1 tablespoon fresh lime juice
- 1 tablespoon fresh lemon juice
- ¼ cup chopped fresh cilantro
- 1 teaspoon mild curry powder (add more for stronger flavor)
- 1 tablespoon paprika
- 1 tablespoon ground cumin
- 1 tablespoon honey
- 1 tablespoon cracked pepper
- 1 teaspoon salt
- 3 cups peeled, seeded, and diced cucumber

1. Mix together all ingredients but the cucumber until smooth and well-combined. Stir in cucumber, cover, and refrigerate. Give it a quick stir before serving.

**Serves 6–8**

# Basic Pasta Dough With Variations

*I have been making pasta for a long time with pasta machines and food processor attachments. My favorite method is to use the food processor to mix the dough and an Atlas pastamaker to roll it and cut the noodles. However, for thick noodles, as for chicken and noodles or beef and noodle stew, I roll out the dough on a floured surface (with a floured rolling pin) to desired thickness, dust with flour, roll up like a jelly-roll, and then slice crosswise. The noodles cook in one or two minutes in a large bath of gently boiling salted water with a tablespoon of olive oil added to prevent them from sticking together.*

> 1½ cups unbleached all-purpose flour
> 1½ cups semolina* flour
> 1 teaspoon salt
> 4 eggs
> 3 tablespoons extra virgin olive oil
> Up to 3 tablespoons water

1. Place both flours and salt into food processor fitted with a steel blade. Add eggs, one at a time, pulsing a couple of times after each one.
2. Turn processor on and add oil in a stream. Slowly add water until a soft, smooth dough is formed. Turn off immediately, flour dough, and wrap tightly until ready to roll.
3. For variety, add ½ cup puréed roasted red pepper, ½ cup finely chopped fresh basil, ½ cup finely chopped parsley, or 2 tablespoons finely cracked pepper before mixing. You may have to reduce or eliminate the water, or even add a small amount of flour to compensate for added liquid.

**Yields: Enough dough for 1 lasagna or pasta for 6–8**

---

* Available at most gourmet shops or Italian specialty stores.

# Caesar Pasta Salad

*This is a great make-ahead luncheon dish which actually improves if made the night before (but no earlier). Serve over shredded Romaine lettuce with slices of garlic bread and white wine and you are all set.*

- **1 2-ounce container of anchovy fillets, drained**
- **½ tablespoon minced garlic**
- **2 tablespoons cracked pepper**
- **1 tablespoon fresh lemon juice**
- **¼ cup fresh parsley**
- **½ cup extra virgin olive oil**
- **16 ounces dried pasta in shape(s) of choice — bows work well — boiled to *al dente*, rinsed in cold water, and tossed with 1 teaspoon olive oil**
- **½ cup chopped sweet red pepper**
- **1 cup marinated artichoke hearts, drained and chunked**
- **1 cup black olives, pitted and sliced in half lengthwise**

1. Place anchovies, garlic, pepper, lemon juice, parsley, and olive oil into food processor fitted with a steel blade and pulse until texture of coarse meal. Add one-eighth of a cup of olive oil and pulse. Repeat three times to use all the olive oil.
2. Place pasta, red pepper, artichokes, and olives in glass bowl. Add the dressing and toss to coat. Serve chilled.

**Serves 6–8**

# Pasta With Walnuts, Garlic And Butter

*One night at our home on the coast of Maine, we stayed up late with friends and got hungry. Having just arrived that day, our supplies were few, and thus our selections limited. I whipped this up and everyone thought it had been planned!*

- ½ cup unsalted butter
- 1 teaspoon minced garlic
- 1 cup chopped walnuts
- 2 teaspoons salt
- 1 tablespoon cracked pepper
- ¼ cup minced fresh parsley, or 1 tablespoon dried
- 1 pound dried pasta (we used angel hair)
- ½ cup grated Parmesan cheese

1. Heat butter in large, heavy sauté pan over medium-high heat until foam subsides. Stir in garlic, walnuts, salt, pepper, and parsley. Sauté for 90 seconds and turn off heat.
2. Boil pasta until *al dente* and drain.
3. Turn heat on walnut mixture to medium-high, stir in pasta and heat for 30 seconds. Serve pronto with the Parmesan on top.

**Serves 6–8 for a light supper or side dish**

# Angel Hair Pasta In Pink Tomato Sauce

*When my wife and new daughter came home from the hospital, I wanted everything pink and perfect. My wife is a pasta and tomato sauce lover, which made my job easy. Later we spiced up the dish, resulting in this recipe. Now our five-year-old daughter loves it too!*

- 3 tablespoons olive oil
- ½ tablespoon minced garlic
- ¼ cup minced onion
- 1 cup sliced mushrooms
- ½ cup chopped sweet red pepper
- ¼ cup chopped fresh basil
- ⅛ cup chopped fresh oregano leaves, or ½ tablespoon dried
- 1 teaspoon salt
- 1 tablespoon cracked pepper
- ½ cup dry white wine
- 2 tablespoons granulated sugar
- 1 cup tomato purée
- 2 pounds fresh angel hair pasta, or dried
- 1 cup crème fraîche*

1. Heat olive oil in deep, heavy sauce pan over medium-high heat and stir in garlic, onion, mushrooms, red pepper, basil, oregano, salt, and pepper. Sauté 3 minutes and stir in wine. Reduce heat to medium-low and stir in sugar.

*Continued*

---

\* Available in most gourmet markets, or you may make your own by combining 1 cup whipping cream with 2 tablespoons buttermilk in glass container. Cover and let stand at room temperature for 8 to 24 hours, or until very thick. Stir well before covering and refrigerate up to 10 days.

2. Reduce heat to low and stir in tomato purée. Allow to cook over lowest heat setting.
3. Boil pasta until *al dente*. Place on hot serving plate.
4. Turn heat under sauce to medium and stir in crème fraîche. Stir for 30 seconds, pour over pasta, and serve.

**Server 6–8**

# Pasta Alfredo

*This is often requested by my daughter and her friends. Why make macaroni and cheese if you were brought up on this? I prefer to add the heavy cream rather than using just milk; this gives the sauce a creamier, more ethereal consistency.*

- ¼ cup unsalted butter
- ½ tablespoon minced garlic
- ¼ cup minced shallots
- 1 teaspoon salt
- 1 teaspoon cracked pepper
- 1 pound dried pasta of choice (fettucine is traditional)
- 1 teaspoon extra virgin olive oil
- 1 cup milk and 1 cup heavy cream, or 2 cups milk
- 4 egg yolks, slightly beaten
- 1 cup grated Parmesan cheese

1. Heat butter in large, heavy sauté pan over medium-high heat until foam subsides. Stir in garlic, shallots, salt, and cracked pepper. Sauté for 2 minutes. Turn off heat.
2. Cook pasta until *al dente*, drain, and return to hot pan. Toss with olive oil.
3. Return heat to medium and add milk (or milk and cream) and egg yolks. Continue to stir until sauce thickens.
4. Stir Parmesan into sauce, then the cooked pasta. Turn heat up to medium-high and cook until contents just begin to bubble. Serve immediately.

**Serves 6-8**

# Pasta Carbonara

The basis for this sauce is cream, eggs, bacon, or thinly sliced ham, and Parmesan cheese. It should be thick and served over piping hot pasta. When a friend at Grinnell College made this for me, I was addicted from that point on. I do not make or order this too often because I just cannot stop eating it. I created this version for my own taste. It is rich and full of bacon, which is no surprise to people who know me well.

- 1 pound minced bacon, or thinly sliced pancetta ham, torn into pieces
- 1 teaspoon extra virgin olive oil
- 2 tablespoons cracked pepper
- ¼ cup chopped fresh parsley
- 1 teaspoon minced garlic
- ¼ cup minced onion
- 1 pound dried fettucine
- 1 teaspoon safflower oil, or other light oil
- 1 cup milk
- 1 cup heavy whipping cream
- 4 egg yolks, slightly beaten
- ½ cup grated Parmesan cheese

1. Over medium-high heat, cook bacon or ham in large, heavy saucepan with olive oil until meat is beginning to crisp. (The bacon will, of course, take much longer than the ham.) Stir in pepper, parsley, garlic, and onion and sauté for 2 minutes. Turn off heat.
2. Boil pasta until *al dente*. Drain and return to pot used to cook pasta and toss with safflower oil.
3. Turn heat under bacon mixture to medium and stir in milk, cream, and egg yolks. Continue to stir until sauce thickens and add cheese and then pasta. Turn up heat to medium-high and cook until sauce just begins to bubble. Serve immediately.

**Serves 6–8 as a side dish or light supper**

# Pasta-Stuffed Peppers

*Here's a fun way to serve pasta. It is ideal for a buffet because it serves easily and is mouth-watering. Surround the stuffed pepper with a vegetable sauté for a very colorful and tempting meal.*

½ cup unsalted butter
2 tablespoons extra virgin olive oil
1 teaspoon minced garlic
2 teaspoons salt, or to taste
1 tablespoon cracked pepper
1 teaspoon dried oregano
¼ cup chopped fresh parsley
¼ cup chopped scallions with greens
1 cup sliced mushrooms
1 cup French green beans, cut into 1-inch pieces
1 cup chopped sweet red pepper
1 pound small pasta bows (farfalle)
8 sweet green peppers*
¼ cup shredded Parmesan cheese

1. Heat butter and olive oil in large, heavy sauté pan over medium-high heat until foam subsides. Stir in garlic, salt, pepper, oregano, parsley, scallions, mushrooms, green beans, and red peppers. Sauté for 3 minutes or until vegetables begin to tender. Turn off heat.
2. Boil pasta until *al dente* (soft to the tooth), drain, and stir into pan with vegetables until bows are well coated.
3. Trim tops off green peppers and remove any seeds from the pepper "cups." Trim small amounts from bottoms if necessary to make pepper cups stand solidly.

*Continued*

---

\* Choose beautiful "perfect" peppers.

4. Divide pasta among peppers and sprinkle with the Parmesan.
5. Arrange stuffed peppers in baking dish and place in preheated 325-degree F. oven for 10 minutes or until hot.

**_Yields: 8 peppers_**

# Veal Sauce

*This sauce is a staple at our home. It is full of browned ground veal, garlic and fresh herbs with a sweet tomato base. To make a quick French bread pizza, smear this sauce hot on a split loaf of French bread, top with Mozzarella cheese and place under broiler until the cheese is hot and bubbly.*

> 2 tablespoons extra virgin olive oil
> 2 pounds fresh ground veal
> 1 pounds sweet Italian sausage, casing removed and discarded
> 1 cup minced onion
> 1 tablespoon minced garlic
> ¼ cup chopped fresh basil
> ¼ cup chopped fresh parsley
> ⅛ cup chopped fresh oregano leaves, or 2 teaspoons dried
> 2 teaspoons salt
> 1 tablespoon cracked pepper
> ½ cup dry red wine
> 3 cups tomato purée
> ⅛ cup granulated sugar
> ½ cup plain breadcrumbs, or more

1. Heat oil in heavy sauce pan over high heat and stir in veal and sausage. Stir to break up meats. Cook over high heat for 15 minutes, stirring frequently to crumble beef and brown evenly until dark brown.
2. Stir in onion, garlic, basil, parsley, oregano, salt, and pepper and reduce heat to medium-high. Sauté for 2 minutes. Stir in wine and reduce heat to medium-low.
3. Stir in tomato purée and sugar and heat until contents begin to simmer. Stir in breadcrumbs if desired.

**Yields: About 6 cups**

# Scalloped Potatoes With Ham

*During my years growing up in Marshalltown, Iowa, our housekeeper prepared this for lunch. Still one of my favorite dishes and now a favorite of my daughter's, this stovetop version is quick and easy, fitting today's lifestyle well. It makes a perfect side dish for fried chicken.*

- **1 cup lean cooked ham, sliced into 1-inch squares**
- **½ cup unsalted butter**
- **2 cups potatoes, peeled, quartered lengthwise and sliced into ⅛-inch wedges**
- **1 teaspoon salt**
- **2 tablespoons cracked pepper**
- **1 tablespoon all-purpose flour**
- **1¾ cups milk**
- **1 tablespoon unsalted butter, melted**

1. Brown ham in large, heavy, ovenproof skillet over medium heat until it begins to brown. Add butter to pan and when it has melted, stir in potatoes, salt, and pepper. Cook, stirring occasionally until potatoes are cooked but still firm, about 12 minutes.
2. Sprinkle flour over potatoes and stir gently for 2 minutes.
3. Reduce heat to medium and slowly stir in milk until contents of pan are thickened. Turn off heat and drizzle melted butter over top. Place pan in oven set on highest setting until top browns. You may also carefully run the pan under the broiler to brown.

**Serves 6–8**

# Shrimp And Scallop Jambalaya

*This is a winner over rice with its full flavor, color, and shellfish. It can be made as spicy as desired by adding ground cayenne pepper or hot pepper sauce. Use fresh shellfish for the best results.*

⅛ cup extra virgin olive oil
1 teaspoon minced garlic
1 cup leeks, sliced into small pieces
2 teaspoons salt, or to taste
1 tablespoon cracked pepper
1 teaspoon hot paprika
1 cup sweet red pepper, sliced into small pieces
½ cup celery, sliced into small pieces
1 cup dry white wine
1 pound fresh shrimp, peeled and deveined
1 pound fresh bay scallops
1 cup tomato purée
1 tablespoon fresh lemon juice
¼ cup mango chutney
1 bay leaf

1. Heat olive oil in large, heavy sauté pan with lid over medium-high heat. Stir in garlic, leeks, salt, pepper, and paprika. Sauté for 2 minutes, then stir in red pepper and celery. Cook for 2 minutes more.
2. Stir in wine and reduce heat to medium. Add shrimp and scallops, tomato purée, lemon juice, and chutney. Add bay leaf, cover, and simmer for 3 minutes or until shrimp are just cooked. Serve immediately.

**Serves 6–8**

*Chapter VI*

# BREADS, COOKIES AND PASTRIES

In Maine, mornings are not complete without a warm breakfast to begin a day of kayaking, canoeing, hiking, fishing, exploring the beach, antiquing, or gallery hopping. When we stay at our Maine home, we love to wake our guests to Caramel Cinnamon Rolls, fresh orange juice and a gleaming bowl of succulent Maine blueberries. With all of us still in pajamas, talking and licking fingers, fond memories rarely fade.

Many people are afraid to bake, feeling it is too complicated. Baking is a breeze. At first, follow recipes carefully. Later you will find yourself creating your own customized breads and pastries.

Cooking, but especially eating, should be fun, not an occasion of stress and agony. Getting comfortable in the kitchen is attained through attitude and practice. So, do not be afraid to try. Rarely is something inedible unless it is burned or raw. Be adventurous — have fun!

*Chapter VI*

# BREADS, COOKIES AND PASTRIES
## Recipe List

*Cheesy Clam Bread*
*Ground Lamb Bread*
*Cinnamon Caramel Rolls*
*Blueberry Muffins*
*Chocolate Pecan Delight*
*Chocolate Fudge Cake*
*Sweet Cocoa Frosting*
*Frangelico Chocolate Buttercream*
*Fruit Tarts*
*Apricot Cheese Balls*
*Coconut Meringues*
*Almond Butter Cookies*
*Bananas Foster*
*Black Bottomed Lemon Meringue Pie*
*Caramel Pecan Chips*
*Almond Date Cakes*
*Vanilla Bean Custard*
*Banana Cake Bread*
*Chocolate Chunk Cookies*
*Peanut Butter Cookies*
*Cream Cheese Brownies*
*Caramel Crisps*

# Cheesy Clam Bread

*A glorious combination of butter, clams, and garlic under melted cheese makes this bread hearty enough for a meal when served with a salad. Offered alongside a pasta dish, it will cause your family or guests to rave, so make plenty. It is quite easy to make, and can be cut into smaller pieces for a casual party.*

- ½ cup butter or margarine
- 1 teaspoon minced garlic
- ½ cup chopped scallions
- ½ cup chopped fresh parsley
- 1 teaspoon dried oregano
- 1 tablespoon dried basil
- 1 cup minced clams, drained
- 1 baguette, about 24 inches long, split in half
- 1 cup shredded Parmesan cheese

1. Heat butter and garlic in large sauté pan over medium-high heat for 4 minutes. Add scallions and heat for 1 minute more.
2. Reduce heat to medium and stir in parsley, oregano, basil, and clams and stir for 2 minutes. Remove from heat.
3. Spoon mixture onto split bread in an even layer and top with Parmesan. Place on baking sheet under hot broiler and watch until cheese bubbles and begins to brown. It must be watched as it will burn quickly after it begins to bubble. Remove from heat and cut each half into quarters. Serve while hot or warm.

**Yields: 8 pieces**

# Ground Lamb Bread

The enticing aroma of this lamb- and cheese-stuffed bread will make your mouth water. Accompanied by a salad with a tangy dressing, this bread makes a satisfying and unusual lunch or supper. It can be slightly cooled, sliced, wrapped in foil, and served warm at a picnic or poolside. Or divide the dough into smaller pieces and bake several smaller "buns." Do not let the thought of baking bread scare you. Breads are fun and easy, especially the stuffed variety. Be the master of your kitchen!

- 1½ cups milk, scalded and cooled to 110°F.
- ½ cup warm water
- 1 package active dry yeast
- 6 cups unbleached all-purpose flour
- 1 tablespoon granulated sugar
- 1 teaspoon salt
- 4 tablespoons extra virgin olive oil
- 2 eggs, slightly beaten and at room temperature
- 3 tablespoons oregano*
- 1 tablespoon safflower oil
- 2 pounds fresh ground lamb
- 1 cup minced onion
- 1 teaspoon minced garlic
- 1 cup chopped red bell pepper
- 1 tablespoon salt
- 1 tablespoon cracked pepper
- 1 cup crumbled or diced feta cheese

*Continued*

---

\* I prefer to use Greek oregano, available at Eastern markets or from Dean & Deluca in New York City.

1. In a large glass or ceramic bowl mix together the milk and water and stir in the yeast to dissolve. Add 1 cup flour along with the sugar, 1 teaspoon salt, 3 tablespoons olive oil, and the eggs. Cover with a damp towel and place in warm spot for 20 minutes or until mixture has doubled in bulk and is like a sponge.

2. Add 4 cups of flour to the mixture along with the oregano and mix with your hands, adding more flour if necessary, until mixture forms a ball. Knead the dough right in the bowl with the ball of one hand until dough is smooth and elastic. Pour 1 tablespoon olive oil over the dough and turn dough to coat with oil. Cover bowl with towel and set in warm place until doubled in bulk, about 90 minutes. Punch down and allow to rise again as before, until doubled in bulk again.

3. During the second rising, heat the safflower oil in a large, heavy skillet over medium-high heat. Stir in ground lamb, onion, and garlic and "scramble" the mixture until the lamb is lightly browned. Stir in the red pepper, salt, and pepper and cook for 2 minutes more. Remove from heat and set aside to cool. Stir in feta cheese.

4. Punch down dough when second rising is completed. Flatten dough on floured surface into a rectangle approximately 20 inches wide and 12 inches high.

5. Spoon the lamb mixture onto the upper two-thirds of the dough. Fold the bottom third of the dough over the bottom half of the filling and fold over again over the top half of the filling to form a sort of jelly-roll.

6. Place on hot stone or on a large, heavy, greased jelly-roll pan, in preheated 350-degree F. oven. Bake until top is brown and sounds hollow when tapped with the back of a spoon. Remove from oven and cool for 10 minutes before slicing. Keep warm and serve as soon as possible.

**Serves 6–8**

# Cinnamon Caramel Rolls

*Picture yourself, on a frosty morning on the bold coast of Maine, waking to the aroma of heavily-cinnamoned, sweet caramel rolls baking in the oven and hot chocolate on the stove. If you do not have a house on the coast of Maine, these sticky buns will taste just as delicious wherever you are!*

> **1 quart whole milk, scalded and cooled to 110° F.**
> **2 packages active dry yeast**
> **8 cups (approximately) unbleached all-purpose flour**
> **2 cups granulated sugar**
> **1 teaspoon salt**
> **4 eggs, slightly beaten**
> **1 teaspoon safflower oil, or other light oil**
> **1 cup butter or margarine**
> **1 cup milk**
> **4 cups light brown sugar**
> **4 tablespoons cinnamon**

1. Place the scalded milk in a large glass or ceramic bowl and stir in the yeast to dissolve. Add 1 cup of the flour along with 1 tablespoon granulated sugar and the salt. Cover bowl with a damp towel and place in warm spot for 20 minutes or until mixture has doubled in bulk and is like a sponge.

2. Mix in the rest of the granulated sugar, the eggs, and all but 1 cup of the flour. Knead with the ball of one hand right in the bowl until a smooth and elastic dough results. You may need to add more flour to accomplish this. Pour the safflower oil over the dough and turn to coat. Cover bowl with towel and return to warm spot until dough has doubled in bulk, about 90 minutes. Punch down dough again, cover bowl, with towel, and return to warm spot.

*Continued*

3. In a heavy saucepan over medium heat, melt the butter and stir in the milk and brown sugar. Continue to stir until the mixture begins to bubble and the sugar is dissolved. Reduce heat to medium-low and allow to simmer for 5 minutes. Remove from heat and set aside.

4. Punch down the dough one more time and, on a heavily floured surface, press dough into a rectangle about 12 inches high and 24 inches wide. Sprinkle with cinnamon. Roll up like a jelly-roll and slice into 12 2-inch thick slices.

5. Generously butter a deep, heavy 14-inch round pan or rectangular 11" x 14" pan and pour in 1 cup of the caramel mixture. Arrange the buns, cut side up, in the pan, leaving a bit of space between them. Pour the balance of the caramel over the rolls and bake in preheated 350-degree F. oven until rolls are brown on top and sound hollow when tapped with the back of a spoon.

6. Remove pan from oven and allow to stand for 5 minutes. VERY carefully, invert pan onto platter by placing platter over pan and quickly turning over together. IF THE CARAMEL GETS ON YOUR SKIN IT WILL BURN YOU!!! USE CAUTION!!! (I learned this the hard way!) Serve hot or warm.

**Yields: 12  6" rolls**

# Blueberry Muffins

These muffins are quick and easy to make. They are bursting with fresh blueberries with a hint of cinnamon. The aroma as they bake makes it difficult to limit consumption to just one. In the unlikely event that you have any left over, wrap them individually in plastic wrap, seal in a zipper-lock bag, and freeze them; then microwave later for a near-fresh taste. They are lovely served with a fruit salad for lunch.

- 2 cups plus 2 tablespoons flour
- 1½ cups granulated sugar
- 1 tablespoon cinnamon
- 1 tablespoon baking powder
- ⅔ cup safflower oil
- 3 eggs, slightly beaten
- ½ cup milk
- 1 tablespoon vanilla extract
- 1½ cup fresh blueberries, picked over, rinsed, and gently patted dry with a paper towel

1. Mix together the dry ingredients except the 2 tablespoons of flour in a large bowl and make a well in the center.
2. Place the liquid ingredients in the well and stir to combine into a slightly lumpy batter. Toss the blueberries with the 2 tablespoons flour and gently fold into batter.
3. Divide batter into paper liners set into muffin pan and bake in preheated 350-degree F. oven until centers of muffins spring back when lightly pressed with a fingertip, about 35 minutes.

**Yields: 12 medium-sized muffins**

# Chocolate Pecan Delight

*The addition of orange juice adds an intriguing citrus tang which is excellent with the chocolate. Don't worry if this dense, fudgy cake rises and then falls a bit — that's normal. After cooling, try placing a doily on top, dusting with confectioners' sugar, and then removing the doily for a delicate, lacy effect. You might also frost with raspberry preserves or serve with fresh strawberries and sweetened whipped cream, but this torte is perfect all by itself.*

- ½ cup unsalted butter
- 2 cups granulated sugar
- ½ cup brown sugar
- 4 eggs
- 1 tablespoon vanilla extract
- 1½ cups unbleached all-purpose flour
- ⅔ cup cocoa powder
- 1 tablespoon baking powder
- ½ cup orange juice
- 1 cup chopped shelled pecans

1. Cream butter, sugars, eggs, and vanilla until lemony color.
2. Blend in flour, cocoa, baking powder, and orange juice.
3. Fold in pecans and pour into greased and floured 9-inch round cakepan wrapped with foil on the outside.
4. Bake in preheated 350-degree F. oven for about 35 minutes or until cake pulls away from side of pan and springs back when gently pressed in center with finger. Cool and remove from pan.

**Serves 6–8**

# Chocolate Fudge Cake

We make this dense, rich chocolate cake frequently. It can be filled and/or frosted, or savored plain with fresh raspberries and mascarpone cheese. I prepare this cake for birthdays, anniversaries, and almost all special occasions. Filling and assembling layers of this cake and then draping with fondant creates a work of art. A filling such as the Frangelico Chocolate Buttercream is hard to beat.

½ cup unsalted butter, softened
½ cup safflower oil, or other light oil
6 egg yolks
2 cups granulated sugar
1 teaspoon vanilla extract
1½ cups all-purpose flour
¾ cup cocoa powder
1 tablespoon baking powder
6 egg whites

1. Cream the butter, oil, egg yolks, sugar, and vanilla. Blend in the flour, cocoa, and baking powder all at once.
2. Beat the egg whites until stiff peaks are formed. Mix one-third of the egg whites into the batter, then fold all of the batter gently into the balance of the egg whites.
3. Pour into 2 greased and floured 8-inch cake pans and bake in preheated 350-degree F. oven on center rack approximately 35 minutes or until cakes pull away from sides of pan and center springs back when gently touched. The cakes will fall slightly when removed from oven and cooled.

# Sweet Cocoa Frosting

*Simple yet delicious, this fluffy delight will fill and/or frost almost any cake superbly. It pipes easily from a pastry bag, but work quickly, as it must remain cold.*

**2 cups heavy whipping cream, very cold
½ cup cocoa powder
½ cup powdered sugar
1 tablespoon vanilla extract**

1. In a chilled bowl using chilled beaters, begin whipping the cream and, while continuously beating, gradually add the cocoa and the sugar.
2. When peaks begin to form, continue beating while adding the vanilla in a stream. Beat until light and fluffy and frosting holds shape when the beaters are pulled from the bowl.

**Yields: About 4 cups**

# Frangelico Chocolate Buttercream

*This heavenly combination has been known to provoke arguments over who gets to lick the beaters. Frangelico liqueur is flavored with hazelnut, a rich nut full of smooth, buttery flavor. Combined with chocolate for a smooth and intense flavor, this buttercream is a crowd pleaser. It's divine on chocolate or white cakes, and will make a scrumptious topping for your favorite lemon cake. And what a superb filling for cream puffs or eclairs!*

> ¾ **cup unsalted butter, softened**
> ½ **cup cocoa powder**
> ½ **cup powdered sugar**
> ⅓ **cup Frangelico Liqueur**\*

1. With an electric mixer, whip the butter while gradually adding the cocoa powder and sugar. As the mixture begins to stiffen, whip in the Frangelico in a thin stream. Whip until mixture is light and fluffy and holds peaks. Use immediately.

**Yields: Just over 1 cup**

---

\* Available at liquor stores.

# Fruit Tarts

*You cannot distinguish these from the gorgeous fruit tarts you see in a fine French bakery, and they are not all that difficult to make. Do not hesitate to make two of these special tarts, as the Pâté Brisée recipe will be enough for two, and you can always use the other one for a spontaneous gift. However, in this case you will have to double the recipe for Vanilla Bean custard. The slightly sweet crust filled with rich custard and topped with fruit makes for a spectacular presentation.*

- **1 recipe Pâté Brisée (see Glossary), chilled, adding 2 tablespoons granulated sugar to the flour**
- **1 recipe Vanilla Bean Custard (see page 196)**
- **2 cups berries, strawberries, blueberries, or raspberries, or combination, trimmed**
- **1 cup apricot preserves**
- **½ cup slivered almonds**

1. Roll one-half of the Pâté Brisée into a circle large enough to cover the bottom and sides of a 9-inch false-bottomed, fluted tart pan. Press firmly into corners. Prick bottom and sides with a fork and press a layer of aluminum foil directly on top of the pastry. Fill with dried beans or pie weights and bake on rack on middle shelf in preheated 350-degree F. oven for 20 minutes. Remove foil and beans or weights and return to oven until crust is browned and crisp. Cool.
2. Fill crust with chilled custard and smooth into an even layer.
3. Attractively arrange berries on top of custard.*

*Continued*

---

* I do this painstakingly one berry at a time, making a circle of alternating berries starting with the outer rim. This takes a while longer, but makes for an absolutely breathtaking tart.

4. Place preserves in small saucepan over medium-low heat and heat until melted and simmering. Using a pastry brush and starting in the center of the tart, cover the fruit with the liquified preserves to glaze. Lastly, paint the top rim of the crust with preserves and gently press the almonds to the preserves to circle the tart. Serve as soon as possible, but may be chilled overnight if you do not mind a slightly softened crust.

**Yields: 1  9" tart**

# Apricot Cheese Balls

*Dried apricots soaked in champagne, sweetened and combined with cream cheese, and finally dipped in chocolate . . . what more could you ask for an elegant combination? These are heavenly served with espresso after a fine meal, and they contribute a festive touch to your holiday table. Arrange on an antique plate and cover tightly with plastic wrap for an impressive gift. Couverture chocolate is made especially for dipping when a thin, even coat of chocolate is desired. It can be obtained at gourmet stores or bakery supply markets.*

> **8 ounces dried apricots, diced**
> **1 cup brut champagne**
> **4 ounces cream cheese**
> **½ cup unsalted butter**
> **1 cup confectioners' sugar**
> **8 ounces real chocolate chips or couverture chocolate**

1. Cover apricots with champagne, refrigerate and soak for 2 to 4 hours. Drain.
2. Cream the cream cheese, butter, and sugar. Fold in the apricots, cover, and refrigerate for 30 minutes.
3. Roll into balls approximately 1 inch in diameter and place on a waxed paper-lined tray. Cover and chill thoroughly in refrigerator, or place in freezer for no more than 20 minutes.
4. Melt chocolate. Dip each ball and return to waxed paper-lined tray. Refrigerate until ready to serve.

**Yields: Approximately 24 balls**

# Coconut Meringues

*These meringues are lightly sweet with a hint of vanilla and a feel of luxury. Crunchy on the outside and somewhat chewy on the inside, these have a delightful texture, due to the addition of coconut. They are perfect for a light dessert, or to take on a picnic.*

>    4 egg whites
>    ½ teaspoon cream of tartar
>    1 cup granulated sugar
>    1 teaspoon vanilla extract
>    1 cup flaked sweetened coconut

1. Beat egg whites with cream of tartar. When mixture begins to get frothy, slowly add sugar. Continue beating until soft peaks form. Still beating, add vanilla in a slow stream and beat until stiff peaks are formed. Fold in coconut.

2. Place heaping teaspoonfuls about 2 inches apart on parchment paper-lined heavy cookie sheets. Bake in preheated 375-degree F. oven for 20 minutes. Turn off heat and allow meringues to remain in oven until lightly browned and crisp to the touch.

3. Remove from oven and peel from parchment paper. Cool on racks and immediately place in airtight container until serving.

**Yields: Approximately 24 meringues**

# Almond Butter Cookies

These are crisp, rich, and delicious, especially with coffee or milk. Easily made, they keep up to five days in an airtight container. They have become one of our Christmas Eve traditions. On that special night, we serve them with hot chocolate for dunking and always leave at least five by the fireplace for Sánta!

1 cup unsalted butter
3 cups brown sugar
1 cup granulated sugar
3 eggs
1 teaspoon vanilla extract
1 teaspoon almond extract
2 cups unbleached all-purpose flour
1 teaspoon baking powder
1½ cups slivered almonds

1. Cream butter, sugars, eggs, and extracts.
2. Mix in flour and baking powder and fold in almonds.
3. Drop by heaping teaspoonfuls about 2 inches apart onto nonstick, heavy cookie sheets.
4. Bake in preheated 350-degree F. oven about 12 to 15 minutes or until edges are brown and centers puff up and also begin to brown.
5. Remove from oven, allow to cool for 5 minutes on tray, and transfer to racks until thoroughly cooled. Store in airtight container.

**Yields: Approximately 36 cookies.**

# Bananas Foster

*Sinfully rich and shockingly easy, this is often requested by family and friends alike. Caramelized bananas served hot over French vanilla ice cream is a difficult combination to beat. It can be flambéed by adding 2 tablespoons of rum just before serving and lighting with a match. Once we took a portable burner on a tailgate and made this, just to watch heads turn!*

½ cup unsalted butter
1 cup brown sugar
1 tablespoon cinnamon
½ teaspoon ground clove
1 teaspoon grated orange zest
1 tablespoon orange juice
1 vanilla bean, cut in half and sliced down the middle
3 ripe bananas, peeled
2 tablespoons rum (optional)
French vanilla ice cream

1. Heat butter, sugar, cinnamon, and clove in large, heavy sauté pan over medium heat until melted and bubbly, stirring constantly. Stir in orange zest, orange juice, and vanilla.
2. Arrange bananas in caramel and sauté for 1 minute. Turn each piece and sauté 1 minute more. If adding rum, pour over the top and ignite with a match.
3. Place scoops of ice cream in serving dishes and spoon bananas and caramel sauce over the top.

**Serves 6-8**

# Black Bottomed Lemon Meringue Pie

*All right, so this is not that easy, but it's well worth the effort. A dessert combining rich, lemony custard with a chocolate pecan crust all under fluffy meringue is reason enough to climb a mountain, and this recipe does not require such an effort. Suitable for just about any occasion, it is best made as close to serving time as possible, as the meringue will weep. You may assemble the custard in the crust and refrigerate, leaving the meringue step for just before serving. I made this during my wife's pregnancy and I turned around to see her finishing off the entire pie. She had meringue on her nose and chocolate around her lips like a little child. She was as iresistible as the pie!*

**Crust**
- 1 cup chocolate wafer cookie crumbs
- 1 cup pecans
- 2 tablespoons cinnamon
- ½ cup unsalted butter, cut into pieces

**Lemon filling**
- 2 cups whole milk
- ¼ cup all-purpose flour
- ¾ cup confectioners' sugar
- 6 egg yolks
- 2 tablespoons freshly squeezed lemon juice
- 1 tablespoon finely grated lemon zest

**Meringue**
- 8 egg whites
- ½ teaspoon cream of tartar
- 2 cups granulated sugar
- 1 teaspoon vanilla extract

*Continued*

1. Place all crust ingredients in food processor fitted with metal blade and process until the texture of corn meal. Press into the bottom and sides of a 9-inch glass pie plate.
2. Combine the milk, flour, confectioners' sugar, and egg yolks in a large, heavy saucepan over medium heat. Stir constantly until thick and slightly simmering. Stir in lemon juice and zest and cook while stirring for 1 minute more. Remove from heat and allow to cool for 30 minutes. Pour into pie crust and refrigerate while making meringue.
3. Beat egg whites with cream of tartar and gradually add sugar while beating to stiff peaks. Beat in vanilla. Spoon onto top of pie filling, sealing the filling by making sure that the meringue touches the crust all the way around. Shape the meringue so that it is like a small mountain and touch and lift the meringue all over to form small, decorative peaks.
4. Place the pie on the lowest shelf in the oven and turn on broiler. Broil until meringue reaches a golden brown and the tips of the peaks darken. Remove and serve within 3 hours, if possible, or refrigerate until serving.

**Serves 8**

# Caramel Pecan Crisps

*These sweet nutty delights are just the right touch after dinner with coffee or espresso. They are easy to prepare and unusual, which makes them a great choice for holiday baking. Fill a tin with these tasty cookies for a wonderful hostess gift.*

> **1 cup unsalted butter**
> **1 cup brown sugar**
> **2 cups granulated sugar**
> **4 large eggs**
> **1 teaspoon vanilla extract**
> **½ cup orange juice**
> **2 cups unbleached all-purpose flour**
> **1 teaspoon baking powder**
> **2 cups chopped pecans**

1. Cream butter, sugars, eggs, and vanilla. Beat in orange juice, flour and baking powder. Fold in pecans.
2. Drop in heaping teaspoonfuls onto heavy nonstick cookie sheets or jelly-roll pans about 2 inches apart.
3. Bake in preheated 350-degree F. oven until brown and crisp, about 20 minutes. Remove from oven, cool 5 minutes and remove to racks.

**Yields: About 36 cookies**

# Almond Date Cakes

*The filling in these small pastries is quite dense and makes them so satisfying for afternoon tea. Serving these morsels on a cold, snowy evening by the fire with some sherry will induce euphoria. The combination of dates with almonds and coconut is deliciously rich and warms the tummy.*

**Pastry**
- 1¾ cups unbleached all-purpose flour
- ¾ cup vegetable shortening, chilled and cut into pieces
- 2 tablespoons granulated sugar
- 2 eggs, slightly beaten and chilled
- ⅛ cup ice water

**Filling**
- 12 ounces pitted dates
- 8 ounces blanched almonds
- ½ cup sweetened flaked coconut
- 2 tablespoons honey
- 1 teaspoon almond extract
- 1 egg white

**Other**
- 1 egg yolk plus 2 tablespoons water
- oil to coat hands to shape filling

1. Place flour, shortening and sugar in food processor fitted with steel blade. Pulse until texture of coarse meal. Process and add eggs in a stream and enough ice water for dough to just begin to gather around blade.
2. Remove dough from blade and quickly knead into a ball, handling as little as possible. Wrap in plastic wrap and refrigerate at least 1 hour or overnight.

*Continued*

3. Place filling ingredients in food processor fitted with metal blade and pulse until coarse but homogeneous.
4. Cut pastry in half and roll on floured surface into 8" x 12" rectangle.
5. Oil hands and form 12–2-inch pucks of filling and arrange in grid on pastry 3 down and 4 across. Beat egg yolk and 2 tablespoons water together and, with pastry brush, paint around each puck.
6. Roll out other half of pastry in a slightly larger rectangle and place over pucks. Using fingertips, press to seal pastry around each puck. Using a decorative rolling cutter or fluted 3-inch tartellete cutter, cut around each puck to form individual cakes.
7. Place on nonstick heavy cookie sheet or jelly-roll pan, brush with remaining egg wash, and slice a small moon shape in top of each.
8. Bake in preheated 350-degree F. oven until golden brown, about 20 to 25 minutes.

**Yields: 12 cakes**

# Vanilla Bean Custard

*Not for calorie counters, this rich custard is ideal for cream puffs or for filling a special cake. Beat it into sweetened whipping cream to make chantilly cream, then serve in champagne flutes topped with fresh berries for a sinful dessert.*

> **2 cups heavy cream**
> **½ cup confectioners' sugar**
> **⅓ cup all-purpose flour**
> **4 large egg yolks**
> **1 vanilla bean, halved down the center**

1. Combine all ingredients in heavy saucepan over medium heat, stirring constantly, until contents begin to simmer. Reduce heat to medium-low and continue to stir for 8 more minutes. Remove from heat and discard vanilla bean.
2. Pour into heatproof glass or ceramic bowl and cover with plastic wrap, allowing wrap to touch the top of the custard. Chill thoroughly.

**Yields: Just over 2 cups**

# Banana Cake Bread

Here's a good way to use bananas that have become too ripe to eat. You may want to double the recipe, since this bread not only is delicious and low in cholesterol, but also freezes beautifully. The intriguing flavor has just a hint of cinnamon.

- **3 cups granulated sugar**
- **¾ cup safflower oil, or other light oil**
- **3 large eggs**
- **1 teaspoon vanilla extract**
- **1 cup skim milk**
- **3 cups all-purpose flour**
- **1 teaspoon baking powder**
- **1 teaspoon cinnamon**
- **3 or 4 ripe bananas**

1. Blend together the sugar, safflower oil, eggs, and vanilla. Mix in the milk and then the flour, baking powder, and cinnamon. Mash the bananas and stir in to distribute.
2. Pour into well-greased 9-inch deep cake pan. Bake in preheated 350-degree F. oven until cake pulls away from sides of pan and center domes up and springs back when gently pressed with fingertip, about 35 minutes.

**Yields: 1 9" cake**
**Serves 8–10**

# Chocolate Chunk Cookies

These are rich and delicious dark chocolate cookies with a crunchy edge and a chewy center. They are easy to make and difficult to resist. If you want to double the recipe, the dough keeps very well for up to four days when tightly covered in the refrigerator. Then bake them fresh as needed, as they are absolute ambrosia when warm. This recipe took four years to perfect and I believe it was well worth the effort.

- 1 cup unsalted butter
- 4 cups light brown sugar
- 1 cup granulated sugar
- 3 eggs
- 1 teaspoon vanilla extract
- ¾ cup cocoa powder
- 2 cups all-purpose flour
- 1 teaspoon baking powder
- 2 cups gourmet chocolate chunks (broken-up dark Lindt chocolate bars work beautifully)

1. Cream the butter, sugars, eggs, and vanilla. Beat in cocoa and then flour and baking powder. Fold in the chocolate chunks to distribute.
2. Drop by heaping tablespoonfuls, about 3 inches apart, onto heavy, nonstick cookie sheets. Bake in preheated 350-degree F. oven until puffy in the centers, even in color and no longer glossy, about 15 minutes. Do not overbake!!
3. Remove from oven, allow to cool for 5 minutes on baking tray and remove to racks with thin spatula to cool thoroughly. Store in airtight container for up to 4 days but best when eaten the same day.

**Yields: About 36 large cookies**

# Peanut Butter Cookies

These cookies are soft in the center, and, as they say about certain potato chips, you can't eat just one! I prefer to use creamy peanut butter for a richer, more delicate cookie, but chunky peanut butter makes an interesting variation. After pressing with the tongs of a fork, try placing a chunk of dark or white chocolate in the center. For Valentine's Day we centered the cookie with a milk chocolate kiss.

- 1 cup unsalted butter
- 3 cups light brown sugar
- 2 cups granulated sugar
- 4 eggs
- 1 teaspoon vanilla extract
- 1 cup peanut butter
- 2½ cups all-purpose flour
- 1 teaspoon baking powder

1. Cream the butter, sugars, eggs, and vanilla. Beat in peanut butter and then flour and baking powder.
2. Drop by heaping tablespoonfuls, about 3 inches apart, onto heavy, nonstick cookie sheets. Press a cross with the tongs of a dinner fork to flatten. Bake in preheated 350-degree F. oven until they begin to brown, about 15 minutes. Do not overbake!!
3. Remove from oven, allow to cool for 5 minutes on baking tray, and remove to racks with thin spatula to cool thoroughly. Store in airtight container for up to 4 days but best when eaten the same day.

**Yields: About 36 large cookies**

# Cream Cheese Brownies

*Fudgy? Chewy? Rich? Yes to all three questions. These brownies are the ultimate flat-style brownie. If you want cake, bake a cake; if you want a brownie, try this recipe.*

- **1 cup unsalted butter**
- **3 cups light brown sugar**
- **1 cup granulated sugar**
- **3 eggs**
- **1 teaspoon vanilla extract**
- **8 ounces cream cheese**
- **¾ cup cocoa powder**
- **2 cups all-purpose flour**
- **1 teaspoon baking powder**

1. Cream the butter, sugars, eggs, and vanilla. Beat in cream cheese and then cocoa, flour, and baking powder.
2. Spread in even layer onto a heavy, nonstick 12" x 17" jelly-roll pan. Bake in preheated 350-degree F. oven until puffy in the center, even in color, and no longer glossy, about 35 minutes. Do not overbake!!
3. Remove from oven and allow to cool before cutting. Cut as needed from plastic-wrapped pan or store in airtight container for up to 4 days (but best when eaten the same day).

**Yields: About 24 brownies**

# Caramel Crisps

*These buttery, lacy cookies are marvelously rich with a distinct caramel flavor. Delicious when served with coffee or hot chocolate, they are also a perfect accompaniment to afternoon tea.*

- **1 cup unsalted butter**
- **2 cups light brown sugar**
- **1 cup granulated sugar**
- **1 teaspoon vanilla extract**
- **2 eggs**
- **1 cup unbleached all-purpose flour**

1. Cream butter, sugars, vanilla, and eggs. Blend in flour.
2. Drop by teaspoonfuls, about 2 inches apart, onto heavy, nonstick cookie sheet or jelly-roll pan. Bake in preheated 350-degree F. oven until browned and thin, about 15 minutes. Remove from oven and cool on tray, removing with a thin spatula to an airtight container.

**Yields: About 3 dozen cookies**

*Chapter VII*

# THE INFLUENCE OF THE ORIENT

Oriental cuisine is not only satisfying to the palate but to our artistic feelings to create. Combinations of sweet/salt, sweet/sour, and hot/sour are limitless. It is a cuisine that can be simple or extremely complex.

Although a wok is perfect for stir-frying, deep-frying and steaming, it is not a requirement. A heavy sauté pan works fine for stir-frying; a large Dutch oven makes a good deep-fryer and steamer. A Peking-style wok from your local Oriental market and a bamboo steamer are utensils you will use repeatedly.

If you have difficulty deciding where to begin, try starting with Sea Jewel Dumplings, then serve Kung Pao Chicken with Dry Fried Beans with Pork. Prepare a large pot of Sweet-Sour Cabbage Stew for a one-dish celebration. The Thrice-Cooked Ribs are a dish that your guests will rave about for weeks, making them well worth the effort.

Simple stir-frys are an excellent way to create low-fat, one-dish meals that make a dieter feel guilty. A little ginger, garlic and soy sauce with some cut-up vegetables and chicken cook quickly in the wok and become a memorable meal with virtually no clean-up. What more could you ask for?

*Chapter VII*

# THE INFLUENCE OF THE ORIENT
## Recipe List

*Candied Shrimp and WonTon Noodles*
*Shrimp In Skin*
*Sea Jewel Dumplings*
*Cellophane Noodles in Black Bean Sauce*
*Hot Sour Soup and Shrimp*
*Szechuan WonTon in Peanut Butter Sauce*
*Pickled Chinese Cabbage With Quail Eggs*
*Steamed Shrimp Balls*
*Pan Fried Dumplings*
*Lobster Lettuce Rolls*
*Thrice-Cooked Ribs*
*Shrimp Spring Rolls*
*Pork or Chicken Lettuce Wrap*
*Thai Noodle Salad*
*Sweet-Sour Cabbage Stew*
*Sprouts in Black Bean Sauce With Garlic and Hoisin*
*Stir-Fry Leeks With Pork*
*Kung Pao Chicken*
*Dry Fried Pork Pie*
*Dry Fried Beans With Pork*
*Homestyle Beef*

*Continued*

*Sesame Noodles*
*Scallion Breads*
*Stir-Fry Vegetables With Shrimp*
*Chicken Stir-Fry On Pan Fried Noodles*
*Candied Shrimp With Scallions*
*Egg Roll-Up With Scallions and Parsley*
*Fried Pudding*
*Almond Cookies*

# Candied Shrimp And WonTon Noodles

*The combination of ginger, garlic, and scallions is classic in Chinese cooking. These heavenly glazed shrimp are enhanced by the crunch of the wonton strips which, when fried, become a crisp noodle. Add some fresh minced lemongrass if you like, or, when the cooking is just completed, stir in some hot oil to spice up the dish.*

- **4 ounces wonton skins, sliced into 1/4 inch strips**
- **2 cups safflower oil for frying wonton strips**
- **1/4 cup soy sauce**
- **1 cup granulated sugar**
- **1/8 cup minced fresh ginger root**
- **1 tablespoon minced fresh garlic**
- **1 cup scallions, cut into 2-inch lengths**
- **1 cup bok choy, sliced into chunks**
- **2 pounds large shrimp, peeled, deveined, rinsed and patted dry**

1. Heat oil in deep, heavy pan and fry wonton strips, in batches, until brown and crisp. Remove to paper towel-lined tray and hold in warm oven.

2. In a wok or large, heavy sauté pan over medium heat, combine soy sauce and sugar and stir until boiling. Reduce heat to medium-low and simmer for 5 minutes. Add ginger and garlic to pan and stirring, cook 2 minutes more. Increase heat to medium-high and stir in scallions, bok choy, and shrimp. Cook until shrimp is just done. Serve over wonton noodles.

**Serves 6–8**

# Shrimp In Skin

These make an appealing appetizer or a mouth-watering addition to dim sum. The garlicky, sesame-gingery combination inside a crunchy wonton skin is exciting and attractive. We make them as a treat on lazy Sunday afternoons just to spice up the day.

> 3 tablespoons sesame seeds
> ½ cup hoisin sauce*
> 2 tablespoons minced fresh ginger root
> 1 tablespoon minced garlic
> 24 medium shrimp, peeled, deveined, rinsed and patted dry (no tails!)
> 24 wonton skins
> ¼ cup water
> 2 to 3 cups safflower oil, or other light oil, for frying

1. In a small, heavy pan over medium heat, stir sesame seeds until lightly browned and toasted. Cool and mix with hoisin, ginger, and garlic. Place in bowl with raw shrimp and stir to coat well.

2. Place one shrimp toward the bottom half of each wonton skin, paint around shrimp with water, and fold over and press to seal. You may fold at a slight angle for a more decorative presentation.

3. Heat oil until very hot but not smoking (test this with a small piece of bread which should turn golden-brown in 30 seconds). Fry wontons in batches until brown, about 3 minutes, cooking long enough for the shrimp to be just cooked (you just might have to try one, what a shame!). Hold on paper towel-lined tray in warm oven until all are fried. Serve immediately.

**Yields: 24 wontons**

---

* In Oriental section at supermarkets.

## Sea Jewel Dumplings

*These dumplings are a treat. Delicate dough, wrapped around morsels of fresh lobster and crab, pan-fried on the bottom until crisp, makes a dumpling of which to dream. The simple dipping sauce combines the flavors of scallions and sesame and causes these jewels to melt in your mouth. Make plenty, because once you start eating them, it becomes very difficult to stop.*

> 1 cup all-purpose flour plus ½ cup for dusting work surface
> ½ cup boiling water
> 24 1½" - 2" chunks cooked lobster meat
> 24 1½" - 2" chunks cooked crab meat
> 2 tablespoons safflower oil, or other light oil
> 2 tablespoons soy sauce
> ⅓ cup chicken stock (see page 159), or water
> 1 teaspoon sesame oil
>
> **Dipping sauce**
> > ¼ cup soy sauce
> > 1 teaspoon sesame oil
> > 1 teaspoon minced scallion greens
> > Hot chili paste to taste (optional)

1. With fork or chopsticks, mix 1 cup flour with ½ cup boiling water until texture of coarse meal. Cover tightly with plastic wrap and allow to rest for 30 minutes. Knead on floured surface briefly until it forms a smooth ball. Roll out on floured surface and cut 24 3-inch circles with a glass or cookie cutter. Keep covered with damp cloth.

2. Working with one circle of dough at a time, place a piece of crab and lobster just below the center of the circle. Paint the circumference with water and fold over sealing tightly with fingertips. You may pinch decoratively to seal but this is unnecessary and more time-consuming. Repeat with all circles of dough.

*Continued*

3. Flour a tray and place the dumplings, not touching each other, on the tray. Cover tightly with plastic wrap and refrigerate until ready for use.

4. Heat the safflower oil over medium-high heat in a large, heavy sauté pan with tight-fitting lid until oil is very hot but not smoking. Arrange the dumplings, not touching each other, in the oil. Fry for five minutes and while frying, mix together the soy sauce and water or chicken stock.

5. Standing back, carefully pour the liquid over the dumplings and quickly cover with the lid. Reduce heat to medium-low and steam-fry for 15 more minutes. Turn off heat, uncover pan, and sprinkle dumplings with 1 teaspoon sesame oil. Mix together sauce for dipping sauce. Serve immediately.

**Yields: 24 dumplings**

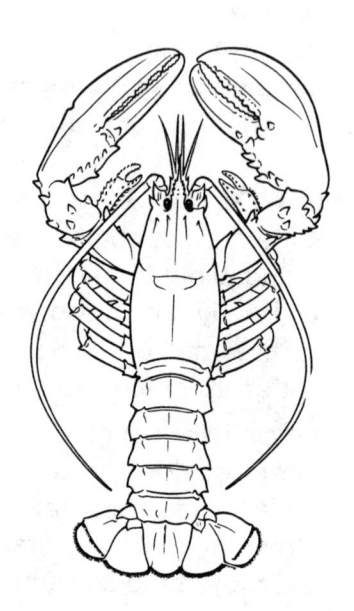

# Cellophane Noodles In Black Bean Sauce

*These fragrant noodles make a delicious accompaniment to Oriental entrees, or grilled meat, fish, or fowl. Add chunks of lobster or shrimp to transform this side dish into a satisfying main course. It's a recipe which is limited only by your imagination.*

**6 ounces bean thread (cellophane) noodles**
**1½ cups chicken stock (see page 159)**
**⅛ cup dry sherry**
**2 tablespoons soy sauce**
**¼ cup thoroughly rinsed and chopped fermented black beans*** 
**1 teaspoon sesame oil**
**Hot oil to taste**

1. Break up the cellophane noodles, rinse, and soak in warm water for 30 minutes, drain.
2. In heavy saucepan with lid, heat chicken stock, dry sherry, and soy sauce until simmering. Add noodles, cover, and simmer for 10 minutes. Stir in beans and simmer for 5 minutes more.
3. Remove from heat, stir in sesame oil and hot oil to taste. Serve.

**Serves 6–8 as a side dish**

---

* In the Oriental section of supermarkets or at Oriental markets.

# Hot Sour Soup And Shrimp

*The hot in this soup comes from hot oil, which may be omitted if you like. Serve this savory broth with shrimp as a hearty overture to an Oriental feast, or allow it to stand alone as a one-dish meal. Homemade chicken stock is preferable, and if several carrots are added to the stock while cooking, it will have a wonderful golden color.*

16 tiger lily buds*
24 dried "wood ears"*
2 cups boiling water
6 cups chicken stock (see page 159)
3 tablespoons cornstarch
¼ cup dry sherry
2 tablespoon rice vinegar
1 tablespoon soy sauce
3 eggs, lightly beaten
1 teaspoon white pepper
½ cup scallion greens, cut into 2-inch pieces
¾ pound cooked cocktail shrimp, sliced in half
2 teaspoons sesame oil
Hot oil to taste

1. Soak the tiger lily buds and wood ears in boiling water for 20 minutes. Trim any tough portions from each and set aside.
2. Heat chicken stock in large, non-aluminum stock pot over medium heat until on the verge of a simmer.
3. Mix together the cornstarch, sherry, rice vinegar, and soy sauce until smooth. Slowly stir into hot stock. Increase heat just enough to bring stock to a slow boil and stir in beaten eggs to feather. Reduce heat to medium-low.

*Continued*

---

* Available at Oriental markets.

4. Stir in soaked and trimmed lily buds, wood ears, white pepper, and scallion greens. Reduce heat to low until ready to serve.
5. When ready to serve, increase heat to medium and stir in shrimp to just heat. Remove from heat and stir in sesame oil and hot oil to taste. Serve immediately.

**Serves 6–8**

# Szechuan Won Ton In Peanut Butter Sauce

These aromatically seasoned wontons are steamed and served from a delicious and rich peanut butter sauce for an outstanding appetizer. The presentation can be stunning with the help of a gorgeous Oriental-style platter, which is all the better if it can be heated. Do not hesitate to try this with leftover fowl.

1½ cups chunked cooked white meat chicken
¼ cup chopped onion
1 teaspoon minced garlic
2 tablespoons soy sauce
2 tablespoons hoisin sauce
1 tablespoon minced peeled fresh ginger
¼ cup chopped cabbage
½ teaspoon five spice seasoning*
1 tablespoon dry sherry
24 wonton skins

Sauce
¼ cup smooth peanut butter
¾ cup chicken stock (see page 159)
1 tablespoon apricot preserves
2 tablespoons hoisin sauce
Hot oil to taste

1. In food processor fitted with metal blade, pulse chicken, onion, garlic, soy sauce, hoisin sauce, ginger, cabbage, five spice seasoning, and sherry until all is minced finely and contents are homogeneous.
2. Place a ball of the filling in the center of each wonton skin. Paint with water and, with fingertips, fold skin over filling at a slight angle and seal, eliminating air.

*Continued*

---

\* Available at most gourmet specialty or Oriental markets.

3. Arrange wontons in steamer (if using a metal steamer, line base with lettuce leaves to prevent sticking) and steam for 10 minutes.
4. Meanwhile, in heavy saucepan, heat peanut butter, chicken stock, apricot preserves, and hoisin sauce over medium heat until smooth and hot but not boiling, stirring constantly. Remove from heat and stir in hot oil to taste.
5. Pour sauce onto large, warmed serving platter and arrange wonton over sauce. Serve immediately.

**Yields: 24 wonton**

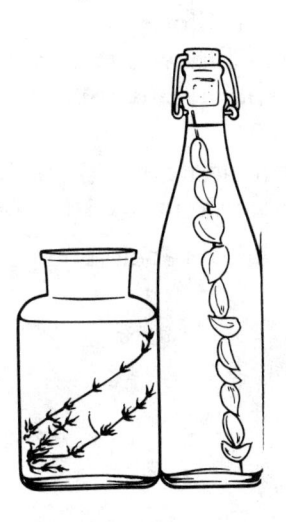

# Pickled Chinese Cabbage With Quail Eggs

Hot and spicy, this could also be named Szechuan cole slaw. Quail eggs are somewhat strong in flavor, and quartered hard boiled eggs may be substituted if desired. However, quail eggs do provoke some interesting reactions and conversation, so try them at least once. They are found in cans or jars at most Oriental markets.

¼ cup rice vinegar
3 tablespoons granulated sugar
½ cup water
1 tablespoon minced fresh ginger
1 teaspoon minced garlic
1 tablespoon soy sauce
1 teaspoon sesame oil
½ teaspoon hot oil or to taste
2 tablespoons hoisin sauce
1 teaspoon cracked white pepper
¼ cup chopped scallions
2 cups chopped Chinese cabbage
24 quail eggs, rinsed and chilled

1. Mix together all ingredients except cabbage and eggs. Toss with cabbage. Refrigerate up to 48 hours.
2. When ready to serve, toss again and gently include eggs. Serve.

**Serves 6-8**

# Steamed Shrimp Balls

*Garlic- and ginger-flavored shrimp balls make an extremely attractive presentation. Disguised with a rice coating, they remain a mystery until tasted, and they are intriguing as a first course or when passed during a cocktail party.*

- **¾ cup minced Chinese cabbage**
- **1 teaspoon salt, or to taste**
- **1 pound shrimp, peeled, deveined and rinsed, patted dry**
- **1 tablespoon soy sauce**
- **1 teaspoon minced garlic**
- **1 tablespoon minced fresh ginger**
- **3 tablespoons minced white onion**
- **1 tablespoon cornstarch**
- **12 ounces glutinous rice**

1. Toss cabbage with salt and set aside for 30 minutes. Place in cheese cloth and wring out the liquid.
2. Place cabbage with balance of ingredients except rice in food processor. Process by pulsing until mixture is finely chopped, homogeneous, and gathering into a well-shaped mass with a texture that allows shaping into balls.
3. Rinse rice in cool water until the water runs clear and spread out onto a sheet of waxed paper. Form the shrimp mixture into 24 more or less uniform balls and roll in the rice to coat.
4. Line a steamer with dampened cheese cloth. Arrange the shrimp balls on the cheese cloth, cover the steamer and steam for 30 minutes from the time steam begins to form. Serve immediately.

**Serves 6–8 as a first course or up to 12 for appetizers**

# Pan-Fried Dumplings

These tasty morsels are found on the menu of most Chinese restaurants because they are so popular, combining the soft dumpling texture with a browned, crispy bottom. They are relatively simple to make and are enhanced to perfection by a simple dipping sauce of ¼ cup soy sauce, 1 tablespoon sesame oil, 1 tablespoon chopped scallion greens, and hot oil to taste.

1 cup chopped Chinese cabbage
1 teaspoon salt
1 cup unbleached all-purpose flour
½ cup boiling water
½ pound ground lean pork
1 teaspoon minced fresh garlic
1 tablespoon minced fresh ginger
1 teaspoon cracked white pepper
2 tablespoons soy sauce
1 tablespoon cornstarch
1 teaspoon sesame oil
2 tablespoons safflower oil, or other light oil
⅔ cup chicken stock (see page 159) or water

1. Toss cabbage with salt, cover, and set aside for 30 minutes. Squeeze liquid from cabbage.
2. With fork or chopsticks, mix 1 cup flour with ½ cup boiling water until texture of coarse meal. Cover tightly with plastic wrap and allow to rest for 30 minutes.
3. Place cabbage with pork, garlic, ginger, pepper, soy sauce, cornstarch, and sesame oil in food processor fitted with steel blade and pulse into a coarse paste.
4. Knead dough on floured surface briefly until a smooth ball is formed. Roll out on floured surface and cut 24 3-inch circles with a glass or cookie cutter. Keep covered with damp cloth.

*Continued*

5. Working with one circle of dough at a time, place a generous teaspoon of the pork mixture just under the center in the middle of the circle. Paint the circumference with water and fold over, sealing tightly with fingertips. You may pinch decoratively to seal but this is unnecessary and more time consuming. Repeat with all circles of dough. Flour a tray and place the dumplings, not touching each other, on the tray. Cover tightly with plastic wrap and refrigerate until ready for use.

6. Heat the safflower oil over medium-high heat in a large, heavy sauté pan with tight-fitting lid until oil is very hot but not smoking. Arrange the dumplings, still not touching each other, in the oil and fry for five minutes. While frying, stand back and carefully pour the chicken stock over the dumplings. Quickly cover with the lid. Reduce heat to medium-low and steam-fry for 15 more minutes. Uncover and continue to fry if all of the moisture is not absorbed, making sure the bottoms of the dumplings are brown and crisp. Serve immediately.

**Yields: 24 dumplings**

# Lobster Lettuce Rolls

*These low fat gems are deliciously refreshing with a delicate tang. They stay fresh up to 12 hours when covered and chilled, making an excellent fix-ahead appetizer for a summer evening cocktail party.*

**12 large outer iceberg lettuce leaves**
**4 cups boiling water**
**1 bowl of ice water**
**1 cup chunked, cooked lobster meat**
**1 tablespoon soy sauce**
**1 tablespoon ginger**
**1 teaspoon sesame oil**
**Hot oil to taste**
**1 cup cooked sticky rice**

1. Trim the lettuce leaves and rinse. Place in colander and blanche with the boiling water. Allow to stand for a minute or two, then immerse leaves in ice water.
2. Toss the lobster meat with the soy sauce, ginger, sesame oil, and hot oil to taste.
3. Divide the rice into 12 clumps and squeeze each clump into a log. Place each rice log at the base of a lettuce leaf and cover with one-twelfth of the lobster, pressing into the rice. Roll up like egg rolls, cover, and refrigerate until ready to serve.

**Yields: 12 rolls**

# Thrice-Cooked Ribs

These are without question the best ribs ever! They are gingery, garlicky, sweet, smokey, and crunchy all in one luscious bite. There are never leftovers — no matter how many are prepared — so stash some ahead of time if you want any for yourself after the party. If time is a problem, buy ribs already smoked from a good barbecue restaurant, but make sure they are not overcooked, as the meat must be firmly attached to the rib bone.

> 2 large slabs lean baby back ribs, smoked and cooled
> 4 cups pineapple juice
> 2 tablespoon sesame oil
> ½ cup soy sauce
> 1 cup cornstarch
> 4–6 cups safflower oil, or other light oil, for frying
> 2 cups granulated sugar
> 2 tablespoons minced fresh garlic
> 4 tablespoons minced fresh ginger

1. Cut the slabs of ribs into individual ribs and, with a sharp cleaver, cut in half any rib over 3 inches long.
2. Mix together the pineapple juice, sesame oil, and ¼ cup of the soy sauce. Marinate the ribs overnight in the mixture.
3. Drain the ribs and coat each one with cornstarch.
4. Heat enough safflower oil in a deep, heavy pan to deep-fry the ribs in 4 batches, adding more oil after each batch to keep ribs submerged while frying. Remove to paper towel lined-tray and hold in warm oven until just before serving.
5. When ready to serve, heat the remaining ¼ cup soy sauce with the sugar in a wok or large, deep pan over medium heat until mixture begins to boil. Reduce heat to medium-low and simmer for 10 minutes. Stir in garlic and ginger and cook 1 minute more. Stir in ribs to coat with sugar glaze and serve immediately.

**Serves 6–8 or up to 12 for appetizers**

# Shrimp Spring Rolls

*Spring rolls are typically lighter and smaller than egg rolls. Traditionally, the wrappers used for spring rolls are derived from rice rather than flour, making a covering that is thin and crispy, and rarely greasy. These rolls have a filling of spicy pork blended with shrimp and fresh vegetables. Assemble them up to twelve hours in advance, then fry just before serving to keep the vegetables crisp.*

1 tablespoon peanut oil
1 pound lean ground pork
1 tablespoon minced fresh garlic
2 tablespoons minced fresh ginger
1 teaspoon cracked Szechuan peppercorns
2 tablespoons soy sauce
¼ cup chopped fresh cilantro
1 teaspoon sesame oil
1 cup shredded Chinese cabbage
¼ cup grated carrot
¼ cup chopped scallions
1 pound fresh small raw shrimp, peeled, deveined and cut in half lengthwise
12 rice paper spring roll wrappers*
1 cup fresh bean sprouts, rinsed and patted dry
4 to 6 cups safflower oil, or other light oil, for frying

1. Heat peanut oil in heavy skillet or wok over medium-high heat and brown pork with garlic, ginger, peppercorns, and soy sauce. When completely browned, the contents of the pan should be dry and very dark. Remove from heat and let stand for 20 minutes to cool.

*Continued*

---

* Available at Oriental markets.

2. Mix cilantro, sesame oil, cabbage, carrot, scallions, and shrimp into pork and divide among bottom of wrappers in a log shape shorter than the wrappers. Divide the sprouts lengthwise along the top of the filling.
3. Paint around the edges of the wrappers with water. Fold ends over filling and roll up to seal.
4. Heat oil in deep pan over medium-high heat until a small piece of white bread turns golden in 30 seconds. Fry spring rolls in batches of 4 until crisp and browned, about 4 minutes. Hold on paper towel-lined tray in warm oven until all are finished. Serve immediately.

**Yields: 12 spring rolls**

# Pork Or Chicken Lettuce Wrap

*This sweet and garlicky filling served inside a crisp lettuce leaf is magical. Quick and simple to make, even in large quantities, it is always a success. Eating it without making a small mess is another story, but well worth it!*

**2 tablespoons safflower oil, or other light oil**
**2½ pounds lean ground pork or coarsely ground white meat of chicken**
**½ cup minced onion**
**2 tablespoons minced fresh garlic**
**3 tablespoons minced fresh ginger**
**2 tablespoons soy sauce**
**1 teaspoon sesame oil**
**¼ cup hoisin sauce**
**Hot oil to taste**
**12 crisp iceberg lettuce leaves**

1. Heat safflower oil in a wok or large, heavy skillet over medium-high heat and stir-fry pork or chicken until cooked and lightly browned. Stir in onion, garlic, ginger, and soy sauce and stir-fry 2 minutes more.
2. Turn off heat and stir in sesame oil, hoisin sauce, and hot oil. Divide among lettuce leaves and serve immediately.

**Serves 6–8 as a first course, 4–6 for an entree**

# Thai Noodle Salad

*This sensational cold pasta dish boasts an intriguing combination of ginger, garlic, and peanut butter, with an element of crunch. It can be made very spicy-hot with the addition of hot oil. When it was on the menu of our restaurant in Tulsa, one regular customer always requested, "Make it so hot that I taste fire." A customer after my own heart, I was happy to oblige.*

- **2 pounds angel hair pasta**
- **2 teaspoons sesame oil**
- **½ cup creamy peanut butter**
- **3 tablespoons soy sauce**
- **⅛ cup safflower oil**
- **⅓ cup hoisin sauce**
- **2 tablespoons minced fresh garlic**
- **3 tablespoons minced fresh ginger**
- **2 teaspoons finely ground black pepper**
- **½ cup chopped fresh cilantro**
- **1 cup fresh bean sprouts, rinsed and patted dry**
- **1 cup freshly cooked, peeled and deveined cocktail shrimp, sliced in half lengthwise**
- **½ cup coarsely chopped dry roasted and salted peanuts**

1. Drop pasta into boiling water and cook until done. Rinse under cold water to cool, drain and toss with sesame oil.
2. Blend together the peanut butter, soy sauce, safflower oil, hoisin sauce, garlic, ginger, pepper, and cilantro. Toss to coat pasta.
3. Arrange pasta in a mound on a serving platter or on individual serving plates. Top with sprouts, shrimp and chopped peanuts. Serve immediately.

**Serves 6–8**

# Sweet-Sour Cabbage Stew

This thick and delicious nonfat soup has a rich, tangy flavor and is perfect for a cold Sunday afternoon. Served with a crusty loaf of bread and a chunk of aged Parmesan, it becomes a meal.

¼ cup whole sesame seeds
1 cup minced white onion
1 cup water
3 tablespoons fresh lemon juice
1 tablespoon salt, or to taste
6 cups shredded white cabbage
2 cups tomato purée
¼ cup chopped fresh parsley
1 cup shredded carrot
1 tablespoon cracked pepper
1 to 1½ cups brown sugar
½ cup unseasoned breadcrumbs

1. In a large, heavy stock pot, toast sesame seeds over medium-high heat, stirring until nicely browned. Stir in onion, water, lemon juice, and salt. Reduce heat to medium, bring to simmer, and stir in cabbage. Reduce heat to medium-low, cover, and simmer 10 minutes.
2. Stir in remaining ingredients except breadcrumbs and simmer 30 minutes more, uncovered, or until vegetables are tender. Taste and adjust brown sugar for flavor.
3. Stir in breadcrumbs to thicken and simmer 10 more minutes.

**Serves 6–8**

# Sprouts In Black Bean Sauce With Garlic And Hoisin

*This is a quick and delicious side dish. Low in fat and high in fiber, it is attractive and aromatic. Top it with sliced grilled chicken for a convenient and healthy one-dish meal.*

**¼ cup light soy sauce**
**2 tablespoons minced fresh garlic**
**1 5-ounce jar black bean sauce***
**4 cups fresh bean sprouts**

1. In a wok or large, heavy sauté pan over medium heat, cook soy sauce with garlic until aromatic. Stir in black bean sauce.

2. Increase heat to high, cook for 1 minute and stir in sprouts. Gently stir-fry for 60 seconds and serve immediately.

**Serves 6–8 as a side dish**

---

\* Available at most supermarkets or Oriental markets

# Stir-Fry Leeks With Pork

Szechuan peppercorns, garlic, and ginger combined with the delicious flavors of leek and browned pork make this dish spicy, but not unbearably so. It is terrific atop chow mein or lo mein noodles and, of course, rice is nice.

- ¼ cup sesame seeds
- 1 tablespoon safflower oil, or other light oil
- 2 pounds lean ground pork
- 2 tablespoons minced fresh garlic
- 3 tablespoons minced fresh ginger
- 1 tablespoon cracked Szechuan peppercorns, or to taste
- 2 tablespoons soy sauce
- 2 cups thinly sliced leeks
- Hot oil to taste (optional)

1. In a wok or large, heavy sauté pan set over medium-high heat, toast the sesame seeds until golden brown. Remove from pan and add safflower oil and pork. Brown pork while stirring to crumble.
2. When pork is browned, stir in garlic, ginger, pepper, and soy sauce, stir-frying for 3 minutes.
3. Stir in leeks and stir-fry for 2 to 3 minutes or until leeks are firm but tender. Remove from heat and add hot oil to taste.

**Serves 6–8 as an entree**

# Kung Pao Chicken

*Peanuts, ginger and garlic . . . a spur-of-the-moment request from a Chinese general inspired the creation of this delectable combination, and the rest is history. Still a classic, it can be made with shrimp, lobster, or pork as well.*

> **5 skinned and boned chicken breasts, 8 to 10 ounces each**
> **3 egg whites, lightly beaten**
> **½ cup dry sherry**
> **3 tablespoons cornstarch**
> **1 large pot of salted boiling water**
> **⅔ cup chicken stock (see page 159)**
> **2 tablespoons soy sauce**
> **2 tablespoons peanut oil**
> **6 Chinese dried red hot peppers, or to taste**
> **3 tablespoons minced fresh garlic**
> **3 tablespoons minced fresh ginger**
> **½ cup chopped scallions**
> **1 cup chopped sweet red pepper**
> **1 cup dry roasted salted peanuts**
> **2 tablespoons hoisin sauce**
> **1 tablespoon sesame oil**

1. Rinse the chicken in cold water and cut up into bite-sized pieces. Mix together the egg whites, sherry, and 2 tablespoons of the corn starch until smooth and milky. Toss the chicken pieces in the mixture, cover, and allow to rest for 30 minutes.
2. Drop the chicken into the boiling water and stir to separate. Boil for 5 to 7 minutes or until chicken is just cooked. Drain, place chicken in glass or ceramic bowl, and cover. (This process is called velvetizing.)
3. Mix together the remaining tablespoon of corn starch with the chicken stock and soy sauce.

*Continued*

4. Heat the peanut oil in a wok set over high heat and stir-fry the hot peppers until they turn black, about 2 minutes. Remove and discard the peppers. Add the garlic, ginger, scallions, and red pepper to the pan and stir-fry for 1 minute. Stir in the chicken and stir-fry for 1 minute more. Now add the peanuts and stir-fry another minute. Stir in the chicken stock mixture and the hoisin sauce and stir-fry until sauce thickens, about 90 seconds.
5. Remove from heat and stir in sesame oil. Serve immediately.

**Serves 6–8**

# Dry Fried Pork Pie

*This brunch or light supper dish could be called sausage and eggs Chinese style. Alternate layers of scrambled eggs and browned pork flavored with garlic, ginger, and Szechuan pepper make an unusual and attractive dish which is served in pie-shaped wedges.*

- **2 pounds lean ground pork**
- **2 tablespoon minced fresh garlic**
- **3 tablespoons minced ginger**
- **1 teaspoon Szechuan peppercorns, or to taste**
- **10 eggs**
- **2 tablespoons soy sauce**
- **3 tablespoons peanut oil for frying egg layers**
- **½ cup chopped scallions for garnish**

1. In wok or heavy skillet placed over high heat, brown the pork until dark brown, stirring constantly to crumble. Stir in garlic, ginger, and pepper and stir-fry for 1 minute. The meat should be quite dry.

2. Beat together the eggs and soy sauce until somewhat frothy. Heat some of the peanut oil in a 12-inch heavy, nonstick skillet with sloped sides over medium-high heat. Pour one-third of the egg mixture into the hot skillet and, after cooking 1 minute, sprinkle one-half of the pork in an even layer over the egg. Cook until bottom is nicely browned. Carefully slide onto a warmed ovenproof serving platter and keep warm in the oven.

3. Make another layer of egg with the balance of the pork and carefully slide on top of the other layer, returning the platter to warm oven when finished.

4. Make the final layer of egg, without pork, and when brown, carefully invert on top of second pork-topped egg layer such that browned side of egg layer is on top. Sprinkle with scallions, cut into pie-shaped wedges and serve immediately.

**Serves 6–8**

# Dry Fried Beans With Pork

*I discovered this dish while riding my bike from classes at Harvard down Mass Avenue to my apartment in Back Bay. I was drawn by a tantalizing aroma into a Szechuan restaurant, where I soon became a "regular." Invariably I would order this dish of crisp green beans with spicy pork, until the staff began bringing it automatically with whatever else I selected. When it came time to leave Boston, I begged the owner and chef to teach me how to make it so I could enjoy it wherever I went. This is a simplified version.*

- **1 pound lean ground pork**
- **2 tablespoons minced fresh garlic**
- **3 tablespoons minced fresh ginger**
- **2 teaspoons cracked Szechuan peppercorns, or to taste**
- **2 tablespoons soy sauce**
- **¼ cup chopped scallions**
- **3 cups safflower oil, or other light oil, for frying beans**
- **2 pounds fresh green beans, rinsed and dried well**
- **½ cup chicken stock (see page 159)**
- **1 tablespoon cornstarch**
- **¼ cup dry sherry**
- **Hot oil to taste**

1. In a wok set over high heat, stir-fry the pork until well browned and dry. Stir in the garlic, ginger, pepper, soy sauce, and scallions and stir-fry for 1 minute more. Remove from wok.

2. Heat safflower oil in wok and, in comfortable batches, deep-fry the beans (any water on the beans will cause the oil to spatter terribly!) until the skin just begins to blister, about 3 minutes per batch. Remove beans to colander set over bowl to drain.

*Continued*

3. Remove the oil from the wok. Return the pork mixture and stir in the chicken stock mixed with the cornstarch and the sherry. Stir-fry until liquid thickens. Stir in the beans and stir-fry for 1 minute.
4. Remove from heat and stir in hot oil to taste. Serve immediately.

**Serves 6–8 as a side dish**

# Homestyle Beef

This delightful entree has an unusual combination of garlic and sweetened citrus. It is absolutely delicious and a lovely dish to serve.

> 1 flank steak, 2 to 3 pounds
> 1 cup fresh or fresh-style orange juice
> 1 tablespoon fresh lemon juice
> 2 tablespoons peanut oil
> ¼ cup soy sauce
> 1 cup granulated sugar
> 2 tablespoons minced fresh garlic
> 2 tablespoons minced fresh ginger
> 3 tablespoons grated or minced orange zest
> 1 cup shredded carrots
> Hot oil to taste

1. Rinse flank steak and pat dry. Cut into chunks that will fit into the pressing chute of your food processor. Place the chunks of beef on plastic wrap and put in freezer for one hour, just to harden but to not freeze solid. Remove beef from freezer and shred on coarse shredding blade of food processor. Toss with orange and lemon juice and allow to marinate for 2 to 24 hours. Drain.
2. Heat peanut oil in wok over high heat and stir-fry beef for 2 minutes, until just lightly browned. Remove from wok.
3. Place soy sauce, sugar, garlic, ginger, and orange zest into unwashed wok over medium heat and stir to combine. When sugar begins to melt, gently stir until contents boil softly, reducing heat if necessary, and cook for 8 minutes.
4. Stir beef and carrots into sugar glaze and stir-fry for 1 minute. Remove from heat and stir in hot oil to taste.

**Serves 6–8**

# Sesame Noodles

A delicate combination of noodles, garlic, and sesame makes these noodles the perfect side dish for grilled meat, fish, or chicken. Serve them in place of rice with Kung Pao Chicken, Home Style Beef, or any other Chinese entree.

> ¼ cup sesame seeds
> 1 tablespoon peanut oil
> 2 tablespoons minced fresh garlic
> ¼ cup soy sauce
> ½ cup chopped scallions
> 6 cups cooked angel hair pasta tossed with 1 tablespoon safflower oil, or other light oil
> Hot oil to taste

1. In a wok over medium-high heat, stir sesame seeds until toasted. Remove from wok.

2. Heat peanut oil in wok over medium-high heat and stir-fry garlic for 1 minute. Reduce heat to medium and add soy sauce and scallions and stir-fry for 1 minute more.

3. Raise heat to medium-high and stir in noodles. Stir-fry for 2 minutes. Turn off heat and add toasted sesame seeds and hot oil to taste, tossing to distribute. Serve immediately.

**Serves 6–8 as a side dish**

# Scallion Breads

*These are crisp, flaky flat breads comprised of many layers, laced with scallions, then toasted on the griddle or in a sauté pan. They have that addictive combination of soy, sesame and scallion which, when dipped into hoisin sauce, becomes an unusual but outstanding appetizer. A Chinese restaurant called ChinChin, located in Manhattan's East Side, makes a wonderful version of these delights and was the inspiration for this recipe.*

**1½ cups warm (110-degree) water**
**1 ¼-ounce package active dry yeast**
**1 tablespoon sesame oil**
**3½ cups all-purpose flour (more may be necessary, depending on humidity)**
**1 tablespoon safflower oil**
**1 cup chopped scallions with greens**
**1 tablespoon soy sauce**
**Oil for grilling**

1. Place warm water in large glass or ceramic bowl and stir in yeast to dissolve. Add sesame oil and 3 cups flour, mixing with hand until smooth ball is formed. Add more flour if needed. Cover with damp towel and keep in warm place for 1 hour.

2. Meanwhile, heat safflower oil in sauté pan over medium-high heat and stir in scallions. Sauté until brown. Reduce heat to medium-low and stir in soy sauce, cooking for 1 minute more. Remove from heat and cool to room temperature.

3. After the dough has risen for one hour, knead the scallion mixture into the dough, adding more flour if needed. Divide dough into 8 small balls and press with palms into ⅛-inch-thick discs. Set aside on floured surface while heating griddle or large sauté pan.

*Continued*

4. Heat a thin layer of oil on medium-high griddle or in large sauté pan over medium-high heat. Brown breads on both sides, about 3 minutes per side, and keep warm until all breads are browned. Cut into wedges, if desired, and serve.

**Serves 6–8 as a first course or up to 12 for appetizers**

# Stir-Fry Vegetables With Shrimp

This delicious, low fat dish is quick and easy, even for large groups. The simple combination of garlic and ginger with shrimp and vegetables is classic and will have your family or guests begging for seconds.

½ cup sesame seeds
1 tablespoon safflower oil
2 tablespoons minced fresh garlic
1 cup chopped onion
2 cups broccoli flowerettes
2 cups snow peas, tips trimmed
1 cup shredded Chinese cabbage
1 cup chopped sweet red pepper
1 cup sliced water chestnuts
2 pounds shrimp, peeled and deveined
2 tablespoons soy sauce

1. In a wok over medium-high heat, stir sesame seeds until toasted. Remove from wok.
2. Heat oil in wok over high heat and add garlic and onion. Stir-fry for 1 minute. Add broccoli and stir-fry 2 minutes more. Add remaining ingredients, including toasted sesame seeds and stir-fry until shrimp are just cooked, about 4 minutes, depending on size of shrimp.

**Serves 6–8 as an entree**

# Chicken Stir-Fry On Pan Fried Noodles

*Here's a one-dish meal that is simple to make and most pleasing to the eye. Cooked pasta is browned in a skillet until it is crisp on the bottom, and then topped with a delicious, low fat stir-fry laced with garlic, ginger and sherry. Enjoy!*

> 5 cups cooked angel hair pasta tossed with 2 tablespoons sesame oil
> 2 tablespoons peanut oil
> 3 tablespoons minced fresh garlic
> 3 tablespoons minced fresh ginger
> 1 cup white onion, sliced into small pieces
> 5–8 10-ounce skinless and boneless chicken breasts, cut into 2-inch chunks
> ⅛ cup soy sauce
> 1 cup snow peas, tips trimmed
> 1 small jar baby corn, drained
> 1 cup chopped sweet red pepper
> 2 cups shredded Chinese cabbage
> ¼ cup dry sherry

1. Press pasta into nonstick, heavy 12- to 14-inch skillet or omelette pan over medium-high heat until it begins to brown on the bottom. Reduce heat to low and cover loosely with foil.
2. Heat peanut oil in wok over high heat and stir-fry garlic, ginger, and onion for 2 minutes. Stir in chicken and stir-fry until just cooked, about 4 minutes.
3. Stir in soy sauce, remaining vegetables, and sherry and stir-fry 1 minute more. Reduce heat to low.
4. Carefully slip noodles onto warm serving platter and cut into 6 to 8 pie-shaped wedges, depending on number of servings desired. Place stir-fry in a mound over noodles and serve immediately.

**Serves 6–8**

# Candied Shrimp With Scallions

*Aromatic and enticing, the delicate combination of sugar, garlic, ginger, and soy sauce makes a superb glaze for the shrimp, which become a stunning, glossy entree. Serve with fried rice or sesame noodles for a small feast.*

**2 cups granulated sugar**
**¼ cup soy sauce**
**¼ cup minced fresh ginger**
**3 tablespoons minced fresh garlic**
**¼ cup grated or finely minced orange zest**
**2½ pounds shrimp, peeled and deveined**
**1 cup sliced scallions**

1. In a wok over medium heat, cook sugar and soy sauce until they begin to bubble. Boil gently for 10 minutes. Stir in ginger, garlic, and orange zest and cook 1 minute longer.
2. Increase heat to medium-high and stir in shrimp and scallions. Stir until shrimp are just cooked, about 3 minutes.

**Serves 6–8 on top of rice or noodles**

# Egg Roll Up With Scallions And Parsley

When I was a child, we hosted a Japanese foreign exchange student in our home. I looked forward to her making "egg roll," and was initially disappointed with these thin layers of egg, filled and rolled up like a jelly-roll. I soon became a fan, however, and realized that the possibilities for fillings are endless. This version uses only scallions and parsley, but use your imagination and add cheese, mushrooms, truffles, herbs, browned ground pork, or anything else your heart desires. Serve surrounded by home style potatoes and toast for brunch.

**8 eggs**
**1 tablespoon soy sauce**
**1 teaspoon cracked pepper**
**2 tablespoons sesame oil**
**1 cup chopped scallions**
**½ cup chopped fresh parsley**

1. With a wire whisk, whip the eggs, soy sauce, and pepper until slightly frothy.
2. Coat the bottom of a nonstick 12- to 14-inch heavy skillet or omelette pan with 1 tablespoon of the sesame oil and heat over medium heat. Pour in just enough egg mixture to coat the bottom of the pan and sprinkle a little of the scallion and parsley over the egg. When the bottom is brown, roll up two-thirds of the egg layer like a jelly-roll and slide to the side of the pan. Pour in more egg to coat the pan up to the flap of the egg and sprinkle with more of the scallion and parsley.
3. Repeat the procedure until all of the ingredients are used up and you have a large, puffy roll of egg which will be golden brown when completely rolled up.
4. Slide egg roll onto a heated serving platter and slice at an angle to expose the fine layers and filling.

**Serves 6–8**

# Fried Pudding

A rich finale to a sumptuous Oriental feast, creamy custard is enclosed in a lightly sweetened crust. Lemon or almond extract can be added to the pudding before frying for additional interest but it is not necessary. To serve, you may flambé with your favorite brandy and douse the flame with chocolate sauce. Counting grams of fat? Get your calculator for this one but it is well worth the splurge!

> 2 cups Vanilla Bean Custard (see page 196)
> 3 egg whites
> ½ cup cornstarch
> ¼ cup confectioners' sugar
> 3-5 cups safflower oil, or other light oil, for frying

1. Spread pudding in an even layer in an 11" x 7" freezer-proof glass dish and place in freezer for 30 to 40 minutes.
2. Meanwhile, beat egg whites until soft peaks begin to form. Continue beating while gradually adding cornstarch and confectioners' sugar.
3. Heat oil in wok or deep pan over medium-high heat until hot.
4. With spoons, form balls of pudding and dip into egg white batter to coat. Drop in hot oil, frying in batches of 4 or 5 just until browned on the outside, about 90 seconds to 2 minutes. Remove to paper towel-lined ovenproof tray and hold in warm oven until all pudding is fried. Serve immediately, dusting with powdered sugar if desired.

**Yields: About 16 puffs**
**Serves 6–8**

# Almond Cookies

*These cookies are delicious — dense and full of almond flavor. Serve them after a Chinese meal on individual ornate plates with handwritten, personalized fortunes. They are delightful with coffee after any meal, or to take as a hostess gift during the holidays.*

½ cup unsalted butter
½ cup vegetable shortening or lard
3 eggs
1 cup brown sugar
2 cups granulated sugar
1 teaspoon vanilla extract
½ cup soft almond paste or marzipan
12 ounces cream cheese
1½ cups unbleached all-purpose flour
1 teaspoon baking powder
36 to 48 whole almonds

1. Beat together the butter, shortening, eggs, sugars, and vanilla until smooth. Blend in the almond paste and cream cheese and finally the flour and baking powder. Cover and refrigerate for 2 to 24 hours.
2. Drop heaping teaspoonfuls of dough onto greased, nonstick cookie sheet lined with aluminum foil on the bottom. Flatten each cookie with the tongs of a fork.
3. Place a whole almond in the center of each cookie and bake in preheated 350-degree F. oven until golden, about 12 to 14 minutes. Allow to cool for 5 minutes before removing to racks to cool thoroughly. Store in airtight containers.

**Yields: 3 to 4 dozen cookies**

*Chapter VIII*

# THE INFLUENCE OF THE SOUTHWEST

My wife, Laurie, having grown up in Mexico City and having spent six wonderful years of our marriage living in Tulsa, Oklahoma, added a special element of the Southwest to our cuisine. Many simple combinations make for great meals like the following recipes for Cacciota and Balck Bean Quesadillas served with Cilantro Pickled Shrimp. Leftover meats and fowl can be chopped, mixed with shredded Jack or cheddar cheese, folded inside a flour tortillas and then grilled for a quick and delicious meal that even kids will love.

There are many great salsas on the market that will do in a pinch, but fresh is always best. A chopped tomato with minced fresh onion, garlic and cilantro and a squeeze of lime is hart to beat, the fresh taste incomparable. Laurie recalls street vendors in Mexico offering fresh peeled jícama sold with sweet or hot chili powder as commonplace. What a simple and healthy, fat-free snack or appetizer!

While in Tulsa, because of its proximity, The Mansion on Turtle Creek Hotel, with its remarkable food, became our hangout. It was there that I had my first warm lobster taco—the rest is history!

*Chapter VIII*

# THE INFLUENCE OF THE SOUTHWEST
## Recipe List

*Homemade Chorizo*
*Chorizo-Tortilla Strudel*
*Tortilla Con Queso*
*Queso Fundido*
*Beans With Bananas*
*Chorizo Sauté*
*Ancho Chile Butter*
*Pepper-Cheese Nachos*
*Black Bean And Corn Salad*
*Jícama Salad*
*Corn Cheddar Muffins*
*Cilantro Pickled Shrimp*
*Cinnamon Fudge Triangles*
*Lobster Quesadillas*
*Tamales Chile Relleno Style*
*Black Beans With Pork*
*Chicken Flautas*
*Bean, Corn and Ancho Chile Caciota Quesadillas*
*Chorizo and Beans With Potatoes*
*Chicken Chalupas*
*Montezuma Pie*

# Homemade Chorizo

The chorizo found in specialty markets is usually a hard-textured variety. The following recipes use chorizo which is more like Italian sausage made fresh by the butcher. When removed from the casing, it can be scrambled and browned to make a base for many Southwestern dishes. Making your own chorizo is quite easy and highly recommended, as this is the only way to know its exact contents and freshness.

> **2 pounds lean ground pork**
> **¼ cup red wine vinegar**
> **1 tablespoon salt**
> **2 tablespoons minced fresh garlic**
> **2 tablespoons mild chili powder**
> **2 tablespoons ground cumin**
> **2 tablespoons cracked black pepper**

1. Mix together the ingredients thoroughly, cover, and refrigerate at least 2 hours and up to 2 days before use. It can also be frozen up to 2 months and thawed in the refrigerator.

**Yields: 2 pounds**
**Serves 6–8 as part of an entrée**

# Chorizo-Tortilla Strudel

*This lightly grilled tortilla filled with spicy chorizo, beans, and cheese can be held in the oven for up to 2 hours, which makes it a great do-ahead appetizer. Slice it at an angle and serve with salsa, sour cream, and homemade guacamole on the side, and your guests will make it into a meal.*

    **2 tablespoons safflower oil**
    **1 pound chorizo**
    **2 tablespoons minced fresh garlic**
    **1 cup minced white onion**
    **1 16-ounce can refried beans**
    **2 tablespoons mild chili powder**
    **2 tablespoons ground cumin**
    **1 cup corn kernels, frozen or canned, drained**
    **½ cup chopped fresh cilantro**
    **6 medium (6- to 8-inch) tortillas**
    **2 cups shredded Jack or mild cheddar cheese**

1. Heat one tablespoon of the oil in a large, heavy skillet over high heat and brown the chorizo while scrambling to break apart. When nicely browned, stir in garlic and onion and stir while cooking for 3 minutes more.

2. Reduce heat to low and stir in beans, chili powder, cumin, and corn, cooking for 1 more minute. Turn off heat and stir in cilantro.

3. Divide mixture among tortillas and fold over like flattened jelly-rolls. Press gently to shape evenly.

4. Heat the other tablespoon of oil in large, nonstick, heavy skillet and brown strudels on both sides. Remove to tray, sprinkle with cheese, and place in warm oven until ready to serve, up to 2 hours. To serve, cut in 1-inch pieces at an angle.

**Serves 6–8 as an entree and up to 14 as an appetizer**

# Tortilla Con Queso

*Few appetizers are easier and tastier than this blend of cream cheese, cilantro, and jalapeño-stuffed olives. Make it a day ahead of time — wrap tightly and refrigerate — and slice just before serving.*

**8 ounces cream cheese**
**½ cup jalapeño-stuffed olives, drained**
**½ cup fresh cilantro**
**¼ cup chopped scallions**
**1 teaspoon mild chili powder**
**4 large (10- to 14-inch) flour tortillas**

1. In food processor fitted with steel blade, process cream cheese, olives, cilantro, scallions, and chili powder until blended, with small chunks remaining for character.
2. Divide cheese mixture among tortillas and spread in an even layer. Fold over as if forming a flat jelly-roll and press gently to even out. Trim ends, if desired. To serve: slice in one-inch pieces at a slight angle.

**Yields: About 36 pieces**

# Queso Fundido

*This dish is a party in itself. If you have a tabletop burner or warming tray, the pan can be set in the center of the table for guests to serve themselves. With some fresh salsa, guacamole, and Mexican beer, you have a complete meal. The spicy pork filling can be combined with many different cheeses; our favorite is an Ancho Chile Cacciotta (see source list) which adds a distinctive flavor to this Southwestern classic.*

> **2 pounds chorizo**
> **3 cups shredded Monterey Jack cheese, mild cheddar cheese, or Ancho Chile Caciotta**
> **12 small (6- to 8-inch) tortillas**

1. In a large, heavy nonstick skillet over high heat, brown the chorizo while scrambling, until almost black. Reduce heat to low and spread browned chorizo into an even layer. Sprinkle the cheese in an even layer over the chorizo. When cheese has melted, serve with warmed tortillas.

**Serves 6–8**

# Beans With Bananas

This is an unusual and delicious side dish for almost any grilled meat, fowl, or fish. It combines black beans with bananas and is laced with cilantro and chili powder. Serve it with warmed flour tortillas as an imaginative vegetarian entree.

> 1 tablespoon safflower oil, or other light oil
> 1 cup minced onion
> 2 tablespoons minced fresh garlic
> ½ cup chopped sweet yellow peppers, seeded
> 30 ounces (2 cans) prepared black beans, drained
> 1 tablespoon mild chili pepper
> 1 tablespoon ground cumin
> ½ cup chopped fresh cilantro
> 2 ripe bananas, peeled and slightly mashed

1. In a large, heavy skillet over medium-high heat, heat oil and brown the onion, garlic, and yellow pepper.
2. Reduce heat to medium-low and add beans to skillet, stirring and pressing with the back of a spoon to mash. Stir in rest of ingredients and simmer until thick and steamy.

**Serves 6–8 as a side dish**

# Chorizo Sauté

*Guests love these gourmet tostadas because they get to choose their own trimmings. Place the crunchy corn tortillas topped with spicy chorizo and beans on a warmed platter or tray. Arrange the garnishes attractively around, then step back to avoid the stampede!*

> 1 tablespoon safflower oil
> 2 pounds chorizo
> ⅛ cup chopped jalapeño peppers, seeded*
> 1 cup chopped onion
> 1 tablespoon minced fresh garlic
> 1 tablespoon ground cumin
> 1 15-ounce can prepared black beans, drained
> 1 cup vegetable oil for frying tortillas
> 12 corn tortillas
>
> **Accompaniments**
> 1 cup each: shredded lettuce, chopped tomato, shredded cheese (choice of Jack, cheddar, and/or Ancho Chile Caciotta), guacamole, and sour cream

1. In a heavy skillet heat oil over medium-high heat and brown the chorizo while scrambling until almost black. Stir in jalapeño, onion, and garlic and cook for 2 minutes more.
2. Reduce heat to low and stir in cumin and black beans. Keep warm over low heat.
3. Heat oil for frying in deep pan over medium-high heat and fry tortillas, one at a time, until browned and crisp. Hold on paper towel-lined tray in warm oven until all are fried.
4. To serve, arrange tortillas on warmed platter or tray and divide meat in center of tortillas. Place in center of table with accompaniments.

**Serves 6–8 as an appetizer or lunch**

---

* ALWAYS wear rubber gloves when handling and preparing hot peppers!!!

# Ancho Chile Butter

*Aromatic and attractive in color, this topping enhances any grilled meat, fowl, or fish. For a mouth-watering entree, sauté shrimp in this mixture and serve with warmed tortillas.*

> ½ **pound dried ancho chile peppers, stems removed and seeded**
> 1 **tablespoon ground cumin**
> 2 **tablespoons mild chili pepper**
> 1 **teaspoon salt**
> 1 **teaspoon sugar**
> 1 **teaspoon minced fresh garlic**
> ½ **cup butter**

1. In food processor fitted with steel blade, process all ingredients except butter until almost smooth, about 2 to 3 minutes. Cut butter into chunks and pulse just until butter is incorporated.
2. Cover and refrigerate until used. Stores up to 1 week.

**Yields: About 1 cup**

# Pepper-Cheese Nachos

These creamy nachos spiked with peppers and onion are a favorite of our five-year-old daughter, Alexa. They can be spiced to taste by your selection of peppers. We use many different types of chips such as black bean, jalapeño pepper, and blue corn. Use your imagination! For a heartier appetite, top with fresh cooked cocktail shrimp, crabmeat, or sliced grilled chicken.

- ¼ cup butter or margarine
- 1 cup chopped onion
- 1 tablespoon minced fresh garlic
- 2 cups seeded, stemmed, and chopped Mexican peppers to taste (sweet yellow cubanelle, jalapeño, and hot banana make a super combination)
- 2 tablespoons unbleached all-purpose flour
- 1 cup milk
- 2 cups shredded mild cheddar or Monterey Jack cheese
- 1 tablespoon ground cumin
- 1 tablespoon mild chili pepper powder
- 16 ounces tortilla chips, spread on a serving platter and warmed

1. Heat butter in large, heavy sauté pan over medium-high heat until foam subsides. Stir in onion and garlic and sauté until onion begins to brown. Stir in peppers and cook for 1 minute. Sprinkle flour over contents of pan and stir for 2 minutes more.
2. Reduce heat to medium and, while stirring, slowly pour in milk. When contents begin to thicken, stir in cheese, ground cumin, and chili powder and continue stirring until sauce is thick and bubbly.
3. Pour sauce over chips and serve immediately.

**Serves 6–8 as an appetizer**

# Black Bean And Corn Salad

*From the buffet table to the supper table, this is a favorite combination. It also makes a refreshing luncheon dish served over shredded salad greens. Beans and corn infused with garlic, cilantro, and sweet red pepper make a deliciously unusual and attractive offering.*

- 1 15-ounce can prepared black beans, drained
- 1 16-ounce can garbanzos, drained
- 1 cup yellow corn kernels, frozen or vacuum packed, drained
- 1 cup diced purple onion
- 1 cup seeded and chopped tomato
- 1 cup chopped sweet red pepper
- 1 teaspoon minced fresh garlic
- ½ cup chopped fresh cilantro
- 2 tablespoons sugar
- 1 teaspoon salt
- 1 tablespoon cracked black pepper
- ⅓ cup red wine vinegar
- ½ cup safflower oil
- 2 tablespoons fresh lime juice

1. Toss all ingredients to mix well. Cover and refrigerate up to three days, stirring occasionally.

**Serves 6–8**

# Jícama Salad

*If you are not familiar with jícama, it is a root vegetable high in fiber with a sweet, crunchy water chestnut-type texture. This refreshing and delicious salad is quite simple to make and very attractive to serve. It is based on a snack that Laurie often had growing up in Mexico City: fresh slices of jícama sprinkled with lime and mild chili pepper powder.*

- **4 cups fresh jícama, peeled and julienned or chunked**
- **2 chopped seeded tomatoes**
- **3 tablespoons fresh lime juice**
- **1 tablespoon granulated sugar**
- **2 tablespoons mild chili pepper powder**
- **2 tablespoons ground cumin**

1. Toss jícama with tomato and lime. While tossing, sprinkle with sugar, chili pepper, and cumin. Serve cold.

**Serves 6–8**

# Corn Cheddar Muffins

*Serve these light, delectable muffins with butter which has been softened and infused with chopped fresh cilantro. They make an excellent accompaniment to the Black Bean and Corn Salad for a fabulous lunch.*

> ½ cup bacon drippings or melted butter
> 5 eggs
> 1 cup safflower oil
> 1 cup sour cream
> 1 cup yellow cornmeal
> 1 cup unbleached all-purpose flour
> ½ cup granulated sugar
> 1 teaspoon baking powder
> 1 tablespoon mild chili pepper powder
> 1 tablespoon ground cumin
> 1 cup yellow corn kernels, frozen or vacuum packed, drained
> 1 cup shredded mild cheddar cheese

1. In a heavy, nonstick muffin tin which holds 12 large or 16 medium muffins, divide bacon drippings or melted butter and place in 350-degree F. oven to heat. Be ready to prepare muffins, as butter will burn after 10 minutes.
2. Beat together the eggs, safflower oil, and sour cream. Blend in the cornmeal, flour, sugar, baking powder, chili pepper, and cumin until a smooth batter is formed.
3. Fold in corn and cheese to distribute throughout batter.
4. Drop batter into hot muffin tins (tins should be about two-thirds full) and bake in 350-degree F. oven until muffins rise, are brown on top, and spring back when gently pressed with fingertip. Serve hot or warm.

**Yields: 12 large, or 16 medium muffins**

# Cilantro Pickled Shrimp

*Not a big fan of raw fish, I came up with this dish as an answer to ceviche. These shrimp are always a hit at cocktail parties and can be served over shredded salad greens for a zesty lunch or light supper. Serve them with the Corn Cheddar Muffins for a real treat!*

**Juice from 6 limes and 1 lemon plus enough water to make one cup**
**½ cup granulated sugar**
**1 cup chopped fresh cilantro**
**2 teaspoons salt**
**1 tablespoon cracked black pepper**
**2 pounds cooked cocktail shrimp, sliced in half lengthwise down the center**

1. Mix together the citrus juice/water with the sugar, cilantro, salt, and pepper. Toss with shrimp. Cover, refrigerate, and marinate overnight or up to 48 hours. Serve cold.

**Serves 6–8 as an entree or salad; up to 12 for appetizers**

# Cinnamon Fudge Triangles

Laced with cinnamon, these fudgy, dense brownies are the perfect ending to a spicy Southwestern meal. They are appropriately festive for the holidays. As an added bonus, they are quickly and easily prepared in a food processor.

- 1 cup butter
- 3 eggs
- 3 cups light brown sugar
- 1 cup white sugar
- 8 ounces cream cheese, softened, room temperature
- 2 tablespoons ground cinnamon
- 1 teaspoon vanilla extract
- 1½ cups unbleached all-purpose flour
- ⅔ cup cocoa powder
- 1 teaspoon baking powder

1. Place butter, eggs, sugars, cream cheese, cinnamon, and vanilla in food processor fitted with steel blade and process just until blended, scraping down sides as needed.
2. Add flour, cocoa, and baking powder to processor and pulse until combined. Scrape down sides and pulse again.
3. Press into greased 12" x 16" heavy jelly-roll pan and bake in preheated 350-degree F. oven on center shelf until contents pull away from sides and center feels firm, about 30 to 35 minutes. Do not overbake.

**Yields: About 60 triangles**

## *Lobster Quesadillas*

One of my best friends claims that this is his all-time favorite dish. These quesadillas are stuffed with grilled lobster and mild cheese, and served with a fresh salsa and guacamole. It's such a luscious combination that I am inclined to put this dish on my top-ten list too!

> **4 large lobster tails, shells removed and deveined, cut in half down the center line**
> **¼ cup fresh lime juice**
> **½ cup soy sauce**
> **2 tablespoons minced fresh garlic**
> **2 tablespoons cracked pepper**
> **⅛ cup olive oil**
> **¾ cup unseasoned breadcrumbs**
> **8 large (10- to 12-inch) flour tortillas**
> **2 cups shredded mild cheddar, Jack or Ancho Chile Caciotta cheese**
> **2 tablespoons safflower oil**

1. Toss lobster tail meat with lime, soy sauce, garlic, pepper, and oil, cover and refrigerate 2 to 24 hours.

2. Drain lobster meat and toss with breadcrumbs. Grill over hot coals until just cooked, turning once. Lobster cooks quickly, no more than 5 minutes to grill!

3. Slice lobster thinly and place slices on one-half of each tortilla. Divide cheese over lobster and fold over tortillas to enclose lobster and cheese (like large tacos).

4. Brush both sides of tortillas with the safflower oil and grill over medium-hot coals just until cheese melts, about 90 seconds per side.

**Serves 6–8**

# Tamales Chile Relleno Style

*While a bit time consuming, this dish can be prepared and assembled the day before and baked just before serving — my idea of easy entertaining. The combination of beef and chorizo, peppers and onions, and a delicious crust and cheese topping is really divine, relished by adults and children alike.*

**2 large white onions, sliced in ½-inch slices**
**1 3- to 4-pound beef brisket**
**3 cups water**
**2 tablespoons salt**
**2 tablespoons cracked pepper**
**2 bay leaves**
**2 cups masa harina**
**1 tablespoon safflower oil**
**1 pound chorizo**
**2 tablespoons minced fresh garlic**
**1 cup chopped white onion**
**2 cups chopped sweet cubanelle banana peppers, seeded and stemmed**
**1 tablespoon mild chili pepper powder**
**2 tablespoons ground cumin**
**¼ cup chopped fresh cilantro**
**3 cups shredded Monterey Jack cheese**
**Sour cream and shredded lettuce for garnish**

1. In a roasting pan with a lid, arrange the onion slices in a layer on the bottom and place the brisket, fat side up, on top of the onion. Pour the water over and sprinkle the salt and pepper over the brisket. Put the bay leaves in the water and cover. Roast in a 325-degree F. oven for 6 to 8 hours, until meat just falls apart. Do not remove lid for first 6 hours of cooking!
2. Remove the brisket to a cutting board and strain the cooking liquid, reserving 1½ cups and discarding the rest.

*Continued*

3. Mix the masa harina with the warm liquid and press into bottom and sides of a large, ovenproof casserole as a crust. Chop the brisket and place in an even layer on top of the crust bottom.

4. Heat the safflower oil in a large, heavy skillet over medium-high heat and brown the chorizo until almost black. Stir in the garlic, onion, and peppers. Cook for 2 more minutes, then stir in the chili pepper and cumin. Remove from heat and stir in the cilantro. Sprinkle the mixture over the brisket.

5. Top the casserole with the cheese in an even layer and bake in a 350-degree F. oven until cheese bubbles and begins to brown, about 30 minutes. Serve hot with sour cream and shredded lettuce.

**Serves at least 6–8 for dinner**

# Black Beans With Pork

*These delicious garlic-laced beans with the rich flavor of roasted pork are fabulous alongside any grilled meat, fowl or fish. The mellow, savory ancho chile-laced Caciotta cheese melted over the top gives a smooth fullnesss and creates an attractive presentation. They can also be served with warm tortillas as a wonderful side dish or vegetarian entrée.*

- **1 2-pound pork roast**
- **2 tablespoons safflower oil**
- **1 cup minced onion**
- **1 tablespoon minced fresh garlic**
- **45 ounces (3 cans) prepared black beans, drained**
- **2 tablespoons mild chili pepper powder**
- **3 cups shredded Monterey Jack, mild cheddar, or Ancho Chile Caciotta cheese**

1. Place pork roast on roasting rack and roast in 325-degree F. oven for 90 minutes to 2 hours or until medium-well done on a meat thermometer. Remove from oven and cool until it can be cut into bite-sized chunks.
2. Heat safflower oil in large skillet over medium-high heat and brown the onion and garlic. Stir in the chunks of pork roast and brown, while stirring, about 2 minutes.
3. Reduce heat to medium-low and stir in beans and chili pepper.
4. Pour into baking dish and top with cheese. Bake in 350-degree F. oven until cheese is bubbly and brown, about 30 minutes.

**Serves at least 6–8**

# Chicken Flautas

Flautas are corn tortillas that are filled and then rolled before they are fired crispy and golden brown. When served topped with shredded lettuce, guacamole and sour cream, they create a meal in themselves. These are filled with marinated grilled chicken tickled with a hint of lemon and flavored with chili powder and cumin. A superb treat.

**4 8- to 10-ounce boneless, skinless chicken breasts**
**⅓ cup olive oil**
**2 tablespoons lemon juice**
**1 tablespoon salt**
**1 tablespoon cracked pepper**
**1 tablespoon medium-hot chili powder**
**1 tablespoon ground cumin**
**3 to 4 cups safflower oil for frying**
**18 corn tortillas**

1. Cut each chicken breast into two pieces and place in zipper-lock plastic bag with olive oil, lemon juice, salt, pepper, chili powder, and cumin. Seal bag, enclosing enough air in bag to shake and coat chicken thoroughly. Marinate for 2 hours or up to 24 hours.
2. Grill chicken over medium-hot flame or coals until just done but still juicy, about 4 minutes per side. Chop or shred chicken.
3. Heat safflower oil in deep, heavy pan over medium-high heat. Place a portion of the chicken in a line near the bottom of a tortilla. Roll up tightly and, holding firmly with tongs, deep fry in the oil until tortilla is golden and crisp, about 2 minutes. Once you are comfortable with the routine, you may use 2 pairs of tongs and do 2 at once. Place flautas on paper towel-lined tray in warm oven until all are completed. Serve hot.

**Yields: 18 flautas**
**Serves 6–8 for an entrée or up to 10 for appetizers**

# Bean, Corn And Ancho Chile Caciotta Quesadillas

*This fabulous combination laced with fresh cilantro will impress your vegetarian friends, and everyone else who tries them too. If you grill them over coals, you have the ultimate treat, but they are also delicious cooked on a griddle or in a skillet.*

2 tablespoons safflower oil
1 cup chopped onion
2 tablespoons minced fresh garlic
¼ cup chopped jalapeño peppers, seeded and stemmed*
30 ounces (2 cans) prepared black beans, drained
2 cups yellow corn kernels, frozen or vacuum packed, drained
1 tablespoon ground cumin
⅓ cup chopped fresh cilantro
12 large (10- to 12-inch) flour tortillas
2 cups shredded Ancho Chile Caciotta cheese

1. Heat 1 tablespoon of the safflower oil in a large, heavy skillet over medium-high heat and brown the onion, garlic and jalapeño.
2. Reduce heat to medium. Add the beans, corn, and cumin, stirring for 2 minutes. Turn off heat and stir in cilantro.
3. Lay out tortillas and divide bean mixture among tortillas. Smooth into an even layer covering exactly one half of each tortilla. Top beans with shredded cheese and fold over tortilla to cover filling.
4. Brush both sides of filled tortilla with remaining safflower oil and grill over medium-high heat until cheese melts and tortilla begins to brown, about 90 seconds per side.

**Serves 6–8**

---

\* ALWAYS wear gloves when handling hot peppers!!!

# Chorizo And Beans With Potatoes

*This is another frequently requested dish. Served with a salad, it is a complete and hearty meal. The spicy casserole is topped with whipped potatoes and cheese, and then baked in the oven. Potato skins surround the casserole for a beautiful presentation.*

**6 large baking potatoes**
**2 tablespoons safflower oil**
**2 pounds chorizo**
**1 cup minced onion**
**2 tablespoons minced fresh garlic**
**1 cup chopped sweet cubanelle peppers, stemmed and seeded**
**2 tablespoons mild chili powder**
**2 tablespoons ground cumin**
**30 ounces (2 cans) prepared black beans, drained**
**½ cup chopped fresh cilantro**
**¼ cup butter**
**3 eggs**
**1 tablespoon salt**
**2 cups broken tortilla chips**
**2 cups shredded mild cheddar or Monterey Jack cheese**

1. Pierce each potato with the tip of a knife a few times and bake in a 325-degree F. oven directly on the rack until soft and tender, about 2 hours.
2. Meanwhile, heat the safflower oil in a heavy skillet over medium-high heat and brown the chorizo until almost black. Stir in the onion, garlic, and banana peppers and cook 2 minutes more.

*Continued*

3. Reduce heat to medium-low and stir in the chili powder, cumin, and black beans, cooking for 1 minute more. Turn down heat to lowest setting and stir in cilantro. Keep warm until potatoes are ready.
4. Place butter in glass or ceramic bowl. When potatoes are baked, using a mitt to handle them, cut in half and scoop out hot flesh into bowl, melting the butter. Reserve the skins.
5. Beat the potato with the butter and whip in the eggs and salt.
6. Place the tortilla chips in the bottom of a large casserole and place the chorizo mixture in an even layer on top of the chips. Spread the potato on top of meat mixture to seal. Cut each potato skin in half again and press, cut side down, around the edge of the casserole to appear as a crust. Spread the cheese over the potato.
7. Bake in a preheated 350-degree F. oven until cheese melts and browns.

**Serves at least 6–8**

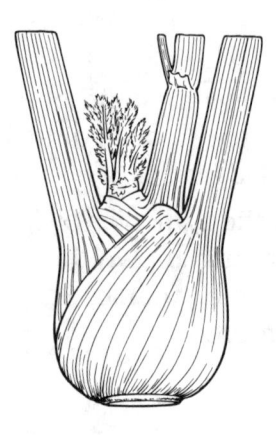

# Chicken Chalupas

Here's a delightful way to use extra grilled chicken or smoked fowl. Of course, it is worth it to cook the meat specifically for this dish, but when grilling for another meal we often prepare extra chicken on purpose so that we can make these treasures the next day with very little effort.

- 1 tablespoon safflower oil
- 1 cup chopped onion
- 1 tablespoon minced fresh garlic
- 1 tablespoon mild chili powder
- I tablespoon ground cumin
- 16 ounces (1 can) prepared refried beans
- 1 cup yellow corn kernels, frozen or vacuum packed, drained
- 2 cups chopped cooked skinless and boneless chicken breasts
- ½ cup chopped fresh cilantro
- 18 corn tortillas
- 1 cup safflower oil for frying
- 2 cups each: shredded Monterey Jack cheese, shredded lettuce, and fresh salsa for garnish

1. Heat 1 tablespoon of safflower oil in large, heavy skillet over medium-high heat and brown onion and garlic. Reduce heat to medium and stir in chili powder, cumin, beans and corn. Cook for 2 minutes.

2. Reduce heat to medium-low and stir in chicken and cilantro. Keep warm while preparing tortillas.

3. Fry tortillas in hot safflower oil until crisp, using tongs to submerge. Drain and keep warm in oven on paper towel-lined tray until ready to assemble.

4. Arrange tortillas on hot serving tray and place a mound of the chicken mixture in the center of each. Top with cheese and lettuce and serve immediately with salsa.

**Serves 6–8 as an entree or 12 as an appetizer**

# Montezuma Pie

*Assemble this delicious casserole the day before and bake it just before serving. It is a meal in itself and makes a striking presentation. It is like a Mexican lasagna, with layers of meat, cheese and beans. Although this version calls for ground sirloin, you could just as well use chorizo, pork loin, or grilled chicken.*

- 2 tablespoons safflower oil
- 2 pounds ground sirloin
- 1 cup minced onion
- 3 tablespoons minced fresh garlic
- ¼ cup minced jalapeño pepper, stemmed and seeded*
- 1 cup tomato purée
- 1 tablespoon sugar
- 1 tablespoon salt
- 1 cup sour cream
- 30 ounces (2 cans) prepared black beans with liquid
- 1 tablespoon mild chili pepper powder
- 2 tablespoons ground cumin
- ½ cup chopped fresh cilantro
- 3 eggs, slightly beaten
- 1 cup oil for frying
- 5 flour tortillas, trimmed to fit a large soufflé dish
- 3 cups shredded mild cheddar cheese
- Salsa and shredded lettuce for garnish

1. Heat safflower oil in large, heavy skillet over medium-high heat and brown beef while scrambling until dark. Stir in onion, garlic, and jalapeño and stir for 2 minutes more. Reduce heat to low and stir in tomato purée, sugar, salt, and sour cream. Keep warm on lowest setting.

*Continued*

---

*ALWAYS wear gloves when handling and preparing hot peppers!!!

2. In a saucepan over medium heat, cook beans with juice, chili powder, and cumin until they simmer. Stir in cilantro and then eggs and stir until contents thicken. Turn off heat.
3. In a deep, heavy pan heat frying oil. Fry tortillas, one at a time, until brown and crisp. Drain on paper towels.
4. Place a tortilla in the bottom of the soufflé dish. Spread one-half of the beef mixture in an even layer on the tortilla and top with one-third of the cheese. Place another tortilla over and spread one-half of the bean mixture on that. Place a third tortilla on top of the beans and cover with the other half of the beef. Sprinkle another one-third of the cheese over the beef mixture. Top with another tortilla and pour in the remaining bean mixture. Place the last tortilla on top and sprinkle remaining cheese over all.
5. Bake in a preheated 325-degree F. oven until hot and cheese is browned and bubbly, about 45 minutes. Serve hot with fresh salsa and shredded lettuce.

**Serves 6–8**

*Chapter IX*

# LIMITED ENGAGEMENTS

A great many fruits, vegetables, and shellfish have specific seasons. We often try to celebrate the height of each season with some good friends by the preparation of a version of a classic dish and a toast of champagne.

During short seasons, most items will be of best quality and less expensive in the middle of their season. Some examples of limited engagements: Maine shrimp in February, fiddlehead ferns in the springtime, stone crab claws in the winter, and Maine blueberries in the summer. Some dear friends of ours, talented artists who live in Maine, know how much we enjoy the tiny sweet Maine shrimp but detest the bitter February weather. Once they purchased several pounds of the delicacy, froze them, and prepared a surprise feast when we visited the next spring. Fine friends indeed!

Look for special items in your gourmet market or ask your supermarket manager to order them or, have a friend ship them to you. A Fiddlehead Fern Sauté or fresh Blackberry Cobbler would surely be a great way to keep your guests talking!

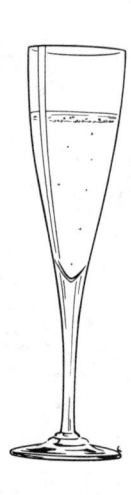

*Chapter IX*

# LIMITED ENGAGEMENTS
## Seasonal Offerings
## Recipe List

---

*Zucchini Blossom And Leek Sauté*
*Fiddlehead Fern Sauté*
*Sweet Maine Shrimp With Garlic and Ginger*
*Carrots With Blueberries And Pistachios*
*Stone Crab Salad*
*Marinated Mussels*
*Fresh Blackberry Cobbler*
*Fresh Raspberry Muffins*

# Zucchini Blossom And Leek Sauté

Zucchini blossoms are found in spring and early summer. In Maine we go to a small produce farm where they let us pick our own. The blossoms are relatively sweet with a faint flavor of the squash. Newly-formed zucchini, if under an inch in length, can be a wonderful addition to the blossom. In this recipe, the blossoms are lightly battered, sautéed in butter, and smothered with sautéed leek for an exquisite flavor and presentation.

- 2 tablespoons olive oil
- 2 cups thinly sliced leeks
- 2 teaspoons soy sauce
- 18 fresh zucchini blossoms, rinsed and patted dry
- 4 eggs, slightly beaten
- 2 cups unseasoned breadcrumbs
- ½ cup butter
- 1 teaspoon minced fresh garlic

1. Heat the olive oil in a heavy skillet over medium-high heat and stir-fry the leeks for 1 minute. Stir in the soy sauce and stir-fry for 1 minute more. Reduce the heat to lowest setting.
2. Dip each blossom in egg and coat with breadcrumbs. Heat butter and garlic in large, heavy nonstick skillet over medium-high heat and sauté the blossoms until golden brown, about 2 minutes per side.
3. Arrange the blossoms on heated serving platter and top with leeks. Serve at once.

**Serves 6–8 as a side dish**

# Fiddlehead Fern Sauté

*The season for fiddlehead ferns is quite romantic, as it signals the birth of spring. For us, the first taste of these delicate shoots after a long winter is solace to the soul. They taste somewhat like mild asparagus and are simply and deliciously prepared with nothing but butter and a little salt.*

**2 pounds fiddlehead ferns, trimmed of tough stems and rinsed**
**1 quart boiling water**
**¼ cup butter**
**1 tablespoon salt**

1. Place the ferns in a colander and douse with boiling water. Drain.
2. Heat the butter in a large, heavy skillet over medium-high heat and when foam subsides, stir in the fiddleheads and salt. Sauté until just tender when poked with the tip of a knife, about 3 to 5 minutes.

**Serves 6–8 as a side dish**

# Sweet Maine Shrimp With Garlic And Ginger

Simple, elegant, and delectable are words that come to mind when considering Maine shrimp. They are not widely served, as their season is in February, but it is worth braving the frigid Maine weather for these sweet and succulent delights. They are the most special of shrimp, and we love them with just a hint of garlic, butter, and ginger.

**½ cup butter**
**1 teaspoon minced garlic**
**1 tablespoon minced fresh ginger**
**2 pounds Maine shrimp**
**1 tablespoon soy sauce**

1. In a large, heavy skillet over medium-high heat, melt butter until foam subsides, then sauté garlic and ginger for 2 minutes.
2. Stir in shrimp and soy sauce and cook just until shrimp are done; 2 to 3 minutes will do. Serve immediately.

**Serves 6–8 as an entree**

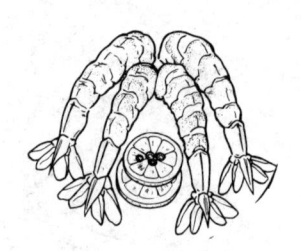

# Carrots With Blueberries And Pistachios

Sweet California-grown carrots, Maine blueberries, and crunchy pistachio nuts make an exciting and colorful combination. It is definitely a summer dish, since that is when the tiny, delicious berries are harvested and shipped throughout the country.

- ½ cup balsamic vinegar
- ½ cup extra virgin olive oil
- 3 tablespoons granulated sugar
- 1 tablespoon cracked pepper
- 3 tablespoons minced fresh shallots
- 1 teaspoon salt
- 3 cups grated sweet carrots
- 1 cup fresh blueberries, picked over and rinsed
- 1 cup shelled salted pistachio nuts

1. Mix together the vinegar, oil, sugar, cracked pepper, shallots, and salt. Toss with carrots, blueberries, and pistachios. Cover and refrigerate up to 4 hours before serving.

**Serves 6–8 as a salad or side dish**

# Stone Crab Salad

*The meat from the stone crab claw is the most sweet and delicate that I have ever tasted. Since it is caught in Florida between October and April, it can be found there during the state's "winter" season. The claws should be purchased and cracked (the fish market will crack them for you) on the day they are to be consumed. Eating them can be messy, so incorporating the meat into a salad is always appreciated by the guests as well as those designated to clean up after the feast.*

> **3 pounds large or jumbo stone crab claws, freshly cracked**
> **1 cup mayonnaise**
> **3 tablespoons Dijon mustard**
> **1 teaspoon sweet paprika**
> **1 tablespoon lemon juice**

1. Pick all of the meat from the claws and place in a glass or ceramic bowl.
2. Mix together the mayonnaise, mustard, paprika, and lemon juice. Toss with the crab meat and serve immediately.

**Serves 6–8 as a first or salad course**

## Marinated Mussels

*We like to walk to our beach in Maine and gather our own mussels for this dish (but only during months with an "R" in them). If you know any martini drinkers, these delectable shellfish go especially well with a very dry gin or vodka martini. Or serve them out of shell over shredded lettuce for a tasty and refreshing salad.*

½ cup extra virgin olive oil
1 tablespoon minced garlic
½ cup red wine vinegar
1 tablespoon sugar
1 teaspoon salt
1 tablespoon cracked pepper
¼ cup minced fresh parsley
⅛ cup minced fresh basil leaves
3 pounds fresh live mussels, rinsed, beard (the hairy clump at the base of the mussel) removed
2 cups white wine

1. Mix together the olive oil, garlic, vinegar, sugar, salt, pepper, parsley, and basil.
2. Place the mussels in a large stock pot with tight-fitting lid along with the wine, and steam over high heat for 5 minutes. Remove from heat and discard any mussels that did not open.
3. Remove mussels from shells and toss with the marinade. Chill up to 12 hours before serving.

**Serves 6–8**

# Fresh Blackberry Cobbler

*Even plain, blackberries seem sinfully indulgent because of their marvelous sweetness and large size. Adding sugar and baking them under a sweet crust, then serving hot with rich vanilla ice cream should be classified a crime of passion.*

**2 pounds fresh blackberries, rinsed and picked over**
**1 cup granulated sugar**
**⅛ cup cornstarch**
**½ recipe sweet Pâté Brisée (see Glossary)**
**1 teaspoon ground cinnamon mixed with 2 tablespoons granulated sugar**

1. Toss blackberries with 1 cup sugar and cornstarch. Place in bottom of pie dish or cobbler dish.
2. Roll out sweet Pâté Brisée to fit over dish and seal berries by crimping pastry to sides of dish decoratively. Cut some small X's or attractive small shapes in top of crust. Sprinkle top of crust with cinnamon sugar mixture.
3. Bake in preheated 350-degree F. oven until crust is brown and crisp, about 35 minutes. Serve warm, à la mode.

**Serves 6–8**

# Fresh Raspberry Muffins

*These sweet muffins are terrific for breakfast or with tea in the afternoon. They are dense and rich, with a hint of cinnamon. We prefer domestic berries to those grown in South America for health and environmental reasons.*

**4 eggs**
**2½ cups sugar**
**1 teaspoon vanilla**
**1 cup safflower oil**
**1 tablespoon ground cinnamon**
**1 cup sour cream or crème fraîche**
**2 cups unbleached all-purpose flour plus 2 tablespoons**
**1 teaspoon baking powder**
**2 cups fresh raspberries, gently rinsed and drained on paper towel**

1. Blend together the eggs, sugar, vanilla, safflower oil, cinnamon, and sour cream or crème fraîche. Mix in 2 cups flour and baking powder.
2. Gently toss the berries with the 2 tablespoons flour and carefully fold into batter.
3. Divide batter into 12 paper-lined medium muffin tins. Bake in preheated 350-degree F. oven until lightly browned and springy when gently pressed in the center, about 35 minutes. Serve warm.

**Yields: 12 muffins**

# ACKNOWLEDGEMENTS

I wish to acknowledge the following people for their contributions in making this book a reality:

To the wonderful photographers, John Southern, Lynn Karlin, and John McCormack. Their work speaks for itself.

To Victor V. and Sharon Ray, who sacrificed their time so that I could be at home cooking.

To our numerous helpers, Lucy Klimec, Julie Bynum, Kathleen Olivo, Zia Lee, Lana Bynum, Bette Lu Dawson, Jane Seibert, Debra K. Smith, and Esther Solzano, who served our guests, and whose help allowed us to relax later while they put our home back in order.

To Miss Gwen at DeHaven's Flower Shoppe in Tulsa, Oklahoma, for the most beautiful flowers imaginable.

To Peter Graham of North Palm Beach, Florida, who encouraged me to finish this book.

To all of our friends and family, whose appreciation made each effort worthwhile.

To W. Richard Young and Joyce LaFray, who believed in me and this very special project.

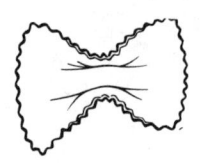

# SOURCES

**For great cheese:**
Mozzarella Company
2944 Elm Street
Dallas, Texas 75226

**For fresh bulk herbs, spices and seasonings:**
Penzey's Spice House Ltd.
P.O. Box 1448
Waukesha, WI 53187

**For quality nuts and dried fruits:**
Sunnyland Farms, Inc.
Albany, GA 31706-8200

**For organic produce and foods:**
Walnut Acres
Penns Creek, PA 17862

**For Southwestern ingredients:**
Los Chileros de Nuevo Mexico
P.O. Box 6215
Santa Fe, New Mexico 87502

Josie's Best New Mexican Foods
2600 Camino Entrada / P.O. Box 5525
Santa Fe, New Mexico 87505/87502

*Continued*

**For unusual and hard-to-find cookware items:**
Rooster Brothers
18 West Main Street
Ellsworth, ME  05605


**For exceptional fudge and homemade candies:**
Al and Pat Blackman
25 Main Street - P.O. Box 267
Clinton, ME  04927


**For fresh honey and beeswax candles:**
Mountain View Apiary
RR1  Box 417
Stockton Springs, ME  04981


**For shortbread and Greek pastries:**
Marika's Kitchen
RR1  Box 209
Gouldsboro, ME  04607


**For eclectic linens and tableware:**
Henri Bendel
712 Fifth Avenue
New York, NY  10019


I'm here if you need me.

Fondly,

Harry

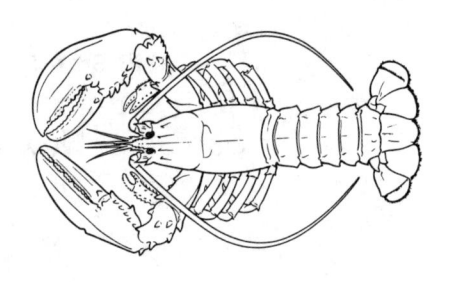

# GLOSSARY

**AIOLI** - A strong-flavored garlic-mayonnaise which is thick and distinctive and used as a sauce, dip or incorporated into other dishes.

**BLINI** - Russian in origin, these pancake delicacies are small in size and made (in this book) of buckwheat and yeast. They can be served with a variety of toppings but often with your caviar of choice and sour cream.

**BRUSCHETTA** - Fine or coarsely chopped tomato, fresh basil, garlic and onion in an extra virgin olive oil served as an appetizer on sliced toasted bread rubbed with fresh garlic.

**BUNDNERFLEISCH** - From Switzerland, this delicacy is air dried beef which has been salt-cured and is served sliced paper thin.

**CACCIOTA** - A cow's milk cheese of Italian origin which has been aged at least two months. It is a mellow and savory semi-soft cheese, similar in texture to Monterey Jack. It can be seasoned with black pepper and garlic, Mexican mint, Mexican oregano, garlic, or ancho chile, mild or hot.

**CARBONARA** - An Italian sauce and accompaniment to pasta, consisting of fresh bacon, cream, Parmesan cheese, fresh garlic and parsley, thickened with a little egg yolk.

**CELLOPHANE NOODLES** - Also known as transparent noodles, these are thin and clear in coloration. They are made from powdered mung beans and when soaked become translucent.

**CHORIZO** - A well-seasoned Mexican polk sausage with flavorings of garlic, chili powder, cumin and other spices. In Spanish cooking, a type of chorizo is made with smoked pork. Casing should be removed and the meat crumbled. One of my favorite uses for chorizo is *queso fundido*.

CILANTRO - A relative of parsley, this fresh, pungent herb is a distinctive seasoning. Quality delicate green leaves should be of healthy coloration.

CROSTINI - A savory, crispy toast that has been fried or dipped into broth. Usually eaten with a topping.

CRUDITÉS - An attractive appetizer array of fresh vegetables which can also include fresh fruits and dried fruits.

ELEPHANT GARLIC - A large white-skinned form of garlic, mild and sweet in flavor.

FETA CHEESE - A goat's milk cheese that is pressed and cured in brine.

FIDDLEHEAD FERN - A spiral-tipped fern that is best consumed when it is about two weeks old. Once it is rinsed, it may be eaten cooked or raw.

FONTINA CHEESE - An Italian cheese made from cow's milk. It has a nutty, yet mild taste.

GARBANZO - Also known as the "Chickpea," this delicate bean is used often in salad and for dips such as *hummus*.

GRATINÉE - Describes a cheese-topped dish baked in the oven or under a broiler which develops a brown, golden crust.

HUMMUS - The primary ingredients are chickpeas, with fresh garlic, extra virgin olive oil and fresh lemon juice. It is often a dip served with chips or crackers or pita bread.

JAMBALAYA - A combination of savory rice, diverse vegetables such as peppers, onions and tomatoes and shellfish, or meat of choice.

JÍCAMA - A Mexican root vegetable which has a light brown exterior and when peeled produces a white, juicy interior to be eaten. The flavor is both nutty and sweet and can be eaten raw or cooked, reminiscent of the water chestnut.

KIWI - Green plum-shaped fruit that is covered with a thick layer of fuzz. Great for garnishing.

PANADE - A thick bread and broth soup. Often defined as a "bread soup," the bread becomes a primary soup ingredient. The dish may be served as a meal in itself. Ideally, a thick, crispy and firm stale bread creates the best flavor and texture by soaking up liquids.

PORCINI - Also known as "cèpes" in France, these wild mushrooms have light brown wide stalks with a cap that is brown and thick. The flavor of the mushroom intensifies as the coloration darkens.

SOUFFLÉ - A dessert or an entree, very light and airy in consistency. The basis for this item is the thick egg yolks by the addition of stiffly beaten egg whites. A soufflé can be sweet, spicy, mild, hot or cold. Generally, hot soufflés are fragile because when removed from a hot oven, the entrapped air escapes which results in deflation.

TABBOULEH - This is a cold salad from the Middle East made primarily of bulgur (cracked wheat) tossed with fresh cilantro, tomato, onion, extra virgin olive oil and fresh lemon juice.

TAPENADE - An Italian concoction consisting of chopped, pitted black olives (preferably oil-cured), capers, oregano, fresh garlic, and a touch of extra virgin olive oil. Served as an appetizer, it is delicious on my homemade toasts.

TORTILLA - A thin, flat pancake-like bread made of dried cornmeal flour, salt and water.

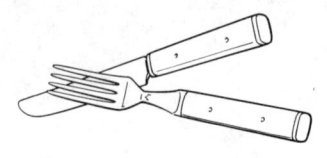

# FROM HARRY'S KITCHEN

BUTTER. I use unsalted sweet cream butter for baking and lightly salted butter for cooking and sautéing.

CHILI PEPPERS (Fresh). A wide variety, from yellow sweet cubanellas to fiery hot cayenne are available. ALWAYS wear gloves to wash, seed and clean peppers.

CHILI POWDERS. These range from sweet and mild to fiery hot. Use according to your own tastes and the tastes of your guests. It is best to use a mild version and place the hot version on the table for individual addition. It is easy to make something more spicy, but almost impossible to make something milder.

CRÈME FRAÎCHE. A very thick, slightly sour cream that does not curdle when heated. It is available at some gourmet stores, but very easy to make. Mix 1 cup heavy whipping cream and 3 tablespoons buttermilk. Cover and allow to stand at room temperature for 10 hours or overnight. It should become very thick. Stir, cover and refrigerate for up to 10 days. Makes 1 generous cupful.

DRIED BEANS, LENTILS AND PEAS. All should be rinsed and picked over before cooking.

DRIED (DEHYDRATED) HERBS, MUSHROOMS AND FUNGI. To rehydrate, rinse them, place in a small heat-proof glass dish and soak in hot water with a tablespoon of cognac for 20 minutes. Drain thoroughly before using.

EGGS. Always use Grade-A large eggs. Bring to room temperature before using. Separate yolk from white in an egg separator, or carefully break shell and pour into cupped fingers, allowing the egg white to drip between fingers into a bowl.

FLOUR. Unless specified, I always use all-purpose unbleached flour.

GINGER. Fresh ginger root is readily available in grocery stores. Peeled and finely minced, it can be soaked in Sherry, covered, and kept up to 10 days in the refrigerator.

PAPRIKA. Unless specified, always use sweet paprika. The hot version really packs a wallop. I use the Hungarian version. Keep in the refrigerator to maintain freshness.

PATÉ BRISÉE. This is a rich, crusty pastry that is easily made in the food processor. For one 9-inch crust (I always make two and freeze one, as they freeze beautifully tightly wrapped in plastic wrap) place 1 cup unbleached, all-purpose flour and ½ teaspoon salt in the food processor fitted with steel blade. Add ½ cup very cold butter or shortening cut into bits, then pulse until the texture of coarse meal. Turn processor on and add up to ¼ cup water in a stream until pastry just begins to form a ball around the blade. Gather into a ball and wrap in plastic wrap. Chill at least 1 hour or overnight. To use, roll on lightly floured surface with floured rolling pin. Add 1 tablespoon granulated sugar to the flour for a sweeter crust.

PEPPERCORNS. I always use freshly cracked pepper; it has a distinctively fresher and more pungent taste. Most grinders can be adjusted from a fine powder to a coarse crack.

RICE. Rice should be thoroughly rinsed and picked over before cooking.

RICE VINEGAR. A clear vinegar found in the Oriental section of most grocery stores.

SALT. Kosher salt, in my opinion, is the best for cooking and baking.

SOY SAUCE. Use a good quality soy sauce. Lite contains considerably less salt.

VEGETABLES. Always wash fresh vegetables and fruits thoroughly before using. Find a source for organic produce for a safer, high quality product. Always trim and chop greens with a stainless steel blade to prevent turning brown.

# Index

## A

Almond Butter Cookies  189
Almond Cookies  241
Almond Date Cakes  194
American Foo Young  133
Ancho Chile Butter  250
Angel Hair Pasta in Pink Tomato Sauce  164
Apricot Bleu Cheese Dip  96
Apricot Cheese Balls  187
Artichoke Tart  46
Asparagus Tips in Pine Nuts  117

## B

Bacon Gorgonzola Vinaigrette  51
Banana Cake Bread  197
Bananas Foster  190
Basic Blintzes  44
Basic Pasta Dough with Variations  161
Basic Quiche with Variations  75
Basil Cheese Toasts  102
Basil Cream Sauce  141
Bean, Corn and Ancho Chile Caciota Quesadillas  262
Beans With Bananas  248
Black Bean And Corn Salad  252
Black Bean Soup  150
Black Beans With Pork  260
Black Bottomed Lemon Meringue Pie  191
Blackened Chicken Breasts  77
Bleu Cheese Balls  116
Bleu Cheese Pie  105
Blintzes, Basic  44
Blintzes, Herbed Cheese  45
Blueberry Muffins  180
Blueberry Rhubarb Chutney  134
Brie with Apricots in Puff Pastry  114
Bruschetta  31
Buckwheat Blinis  129
Bunderfleisch Scallion Rolls  109
Burgers, English  15

## C

Caesar Dressing, Eggless  54
Caesar Pasta Salad  162
Candied Lamb in Phyllo  103
Candied Shrimp  140
Candied Shrimp and WonTon Noodles  205
Candied Shrimp With Scallions  238
Caramel Crisps  201
Caramel Pecan Chips  193
Caramelized Potatoes  67
Carrots with Blueberries and Pistachios  273
Cauliflower Salad  59
Caviar Cucumber Salad  124
Caviar Egg Salad  121
Cellophane Noodles in Black Bean Sauce  209
Cheddar Pea Salad  66
Cheesy Clam Bread  175
Cheesy Spinach  68
Chicken Chalupas  265
Chicken Drumsticks  99
Chicken Flautas  261
Chicken, Grilled With Lemon Sauce  10
Chicken Livers, Italian Style  34
Chicken Liver Omelette  142
Chicken Liver Pâté with Cognac, Apple, and Truffle  58
Chicken Salad Louisiana  69
Chicken, Sesame Sandwiches  18
Chicken Stir-Fry On Pan Fried Noodles  237
Chicken Stock  159
Chili Fried Chicken  7
Chocolate Almond Bars  25
Chocolate Caramel Fondue  72
Chocolate Chunk Cookies  198
Chocolate Fudge Cake  182
Chocolate Pecan Delight  181
Chorizo and Beans With Potatoes  263
Chorizo Sauté  249
Chorizo-Tortilla Strudel  245
Cilantro Pickled Shrimp  255
Cinnamon Caramel Rolls  178
Cinnamon Fudge Triangles  256
Clam Stuffed Chicken Breasts  137
Clam Stuffed Mushrooms  91
Club, Georgetown  17
Coconut Meringues  188
Cold Stuffed Lobster Tails  136
Corn Cheddar Muffins  254
Crab Cakes With Purple Peppers  13
Crabmeat and Asparagus Soup  148
Cream Cheese Brownies  200
Creamy Carrot Salad  126
Crêpes and Variations  143
Cucumber Soup  160
Cucumber Tea Sandwiches  160

## D

Dry Fried Beans With Pork  230
Dry Fried Pork Pie  229

## E

Egg Roll-Up With Scallions and Parsley  239
Eggplant, Stuffed  41
Eggless Caesar Dressing  54
Endive and Lupini Bean Salad  63
English Burgers  15

## F

Fiddlehead Fern Sauté  271
Frangelico Chocolate Buttercream  184
Fresh Blackberry Cobbler  276
Fresh Lemonade  27
Fried Pudding  240
Fried Soufflé  147
Fried Yam Chips  20
Fruit Tarts  185

## G

Garlic Garbanzo Vinaigrette  52
Garlic Parmesan Vinaigrette  50
Georgetown Club  17
Gingered Carrots  62
Goat Cheese Salad, Toasted  32
Goat Cheese Tart with Caramelized Onions  93
Grilled Greens  23
Grilled Vegetables  22
Grilled Lobster  11
Ground Lamb Bread  176
Guacamole Tacos  8

## H

Hearty Vegetable Soup  156
Herbed Cheese Blintzes  45
Herbed Scallops with Smoked Salmon  140
Homemade Chorizo  244
Homestyle Beef  232
Honey Lemon Dressing  53
Hot Ginger Sauce  101
Hot Sour Soup and Shrimp  210
Hummus  95
Husk Grilled Sweet Corn  21

## I

Indian Tuna Salad  61
Italian Salad  55
Italian Style Chicken Livers  34
Italian White Bean Salad  122

## J, K, L

Jícama Salad  253
Kung Pao Chicken  227
Layer Bars  24
Lemon Shrimp in Grape Leaves  37
Lemonade, Fresh  27
Lobster, Grilled  11
Lobster Lettuce Rolls  218
Lobster Quesadillas  257
Lobster Rolls  12
Lobster Soup  149
London Broil Sandwiches  9
Lupini Bean Salad  123

## M

Marinated Artichokes with Mushrooms  48
Marinated Goat Cheese  108
Marinated Mussels  275
Marinated Sweet Peppers  106
Mediterranean Salad  47
Miami Sandwiches  16
Montezuma Pie  266

## O, P

Olive Sauté  36
Pan Fried Dumplings  216
Pasta Alfredo  166
Pasta Carbonara  167
Pasta Stuffed Peppers  168
Pasta with Walnuts, Garlic and Butter  163
Peanut Butter Cookies  199
Pepper-Cheese Nachos  251
Phyllo Pastry with Feta and Spinach  73
Pickled Chinese Cabbage With Quail Eggs  214
Pineapple Crab Mousse  107
Poached Pears and Variations  144
Pork or Chicken Lettuce Wrap  222
Potato, New Salad  19
Potato Pancakes  128
Potato Soup  155
Potatoes, Spinich Stuffed, 43

Poulet Suisse  82
Pumpernickel Pizzas  125

## Q, R

Queso Fundido  247
Rasberries In Rasberry Iced Tea  26
Red and White Cabbage Relish  120
Red Veal with Scallops  80
Roasted Garlic Goat Cheese Tart  92

## S

Salad, Cauliflower  59
Salad, Caviar Cucumber  58
Salad, Caviar Egg  58
Salad, Indian Tuna  61
Salad, Italian  55
Salad, Tabbouleh Pepper  57
Salad, Tuna Pignolia  60
Sandwiches, Miami  7
Sandwiches, Vegetable  64
Scallion Breads  234
Scalloped Potatoes with Ham  171
Scallops in the Shell  39
Sea Jewel Dumplings  207
Sesame Chicken Sandwiches  18
Sesame Noodles  233
Sherried Clam Chowder  157
Shrimp and Scallop Jambalaya  172
Shrimp In Skin  206
Shrimp Spring Rolls  220
Smoked Oyster Pâté  98
Smoked Salmon Pâté  97
Spinach Pancakes  127
Spinach Soup  158
Spinach Stuffed Potatoes  43
Sprouts in Black Bean Sauce With
    Garlic and Hoisin  225
Steamed Shrimp Balls  215
Stir-Fry Leeks With Pork  226
Stir-Fry Vegetables With Shrimp  236
Stone Crab Salad  274
Stuffed Dipped Apricots  135
Stuffed Eggplant  41
Stuffed Mushroom Caps  89
Stuffed Sirloin Roll  139
Sweet Cocoa Frosting  183
Sweet Maine Shrimp with Garlic and
    Ginger  272
Sweet-Sour Cabbage Stew  224
Swiss Cheese Potatoes  71
Szechuan WonTon in Peanut Butter
    Sauce  212

## T

Tabbouleh Pepper Salad  57
Tamales Chile Relleno Style  258
Tapenade  113
Thai Noodle Salad  223
Three Cheese Torte  111
Three Onion Panade  153
Three Onion Soup Gratinée  151
Thrice-Cooked Ribs  219
Toasted Goat Cheese Salad  32
Toasted Onion Chicken  132
Tortilla Con Queso  246
Tuna Antipasto  110
Tuna Pignolia Salad  60
Twice Baked Potatoes  70

## V

Vanilla Bean Custard  196
Veal Sauce  170
Veal with Artichokes and Capers  78
Veal with Prosciutto  84
Vegetable Sandwiches  64

## W

Whole Beef Tenderloin with Raspberry
    Sauce  130
WonTon Noodles  140

## Z

Zucchini and Porcini  49
Zucchini Blossom and Leek Sauté  270

## ABOUT THE AUTHOR

Harry W. Schwartz was born in Iowa and has been cooking since the age of five. He was educated at Grinnell College and George Washington University with post-graduate studies at Harvard University.

Harry and his wife Laurie founded Back Bay Gourmet, a successful Tulsa, Oklahoma restaurant, that was sold only six months after opening. He soon founded Felini's Cookies, another successful operation. He was instrumental in founding the restaurant at Tulsa's Philbrook Museum of Art, and has chaired countless fundraisers.

Currently Harry operates a successful catering restaurant and market, *Surf and Sky Cuisine* in Juno Beach, Florida.

A significant portion of the proceeds from this book will be donated to charity.